Ancient Mandala

Captivitying Coloring Book

ExpertAuthor BluePrint

2015 Copyright Year

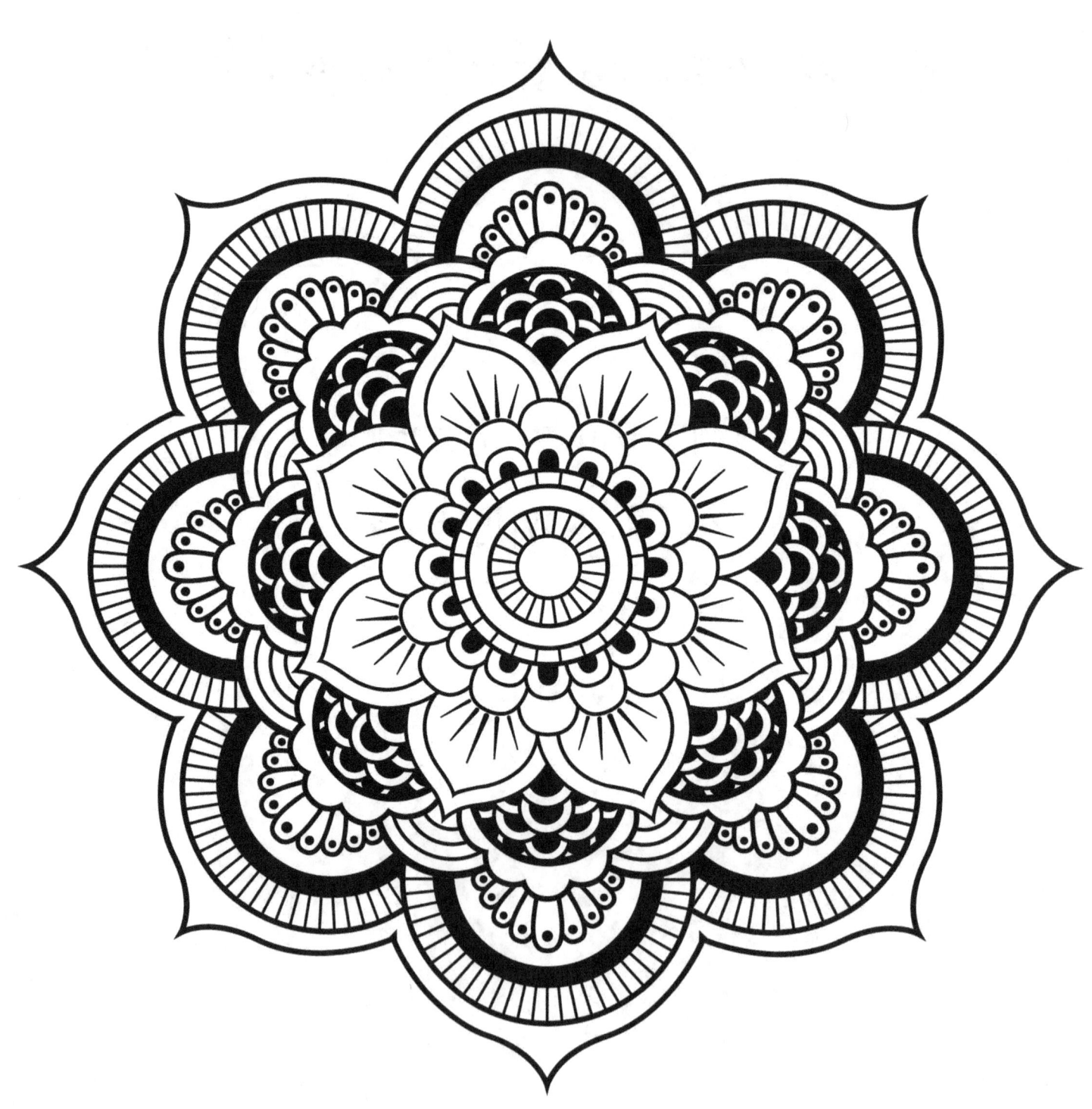

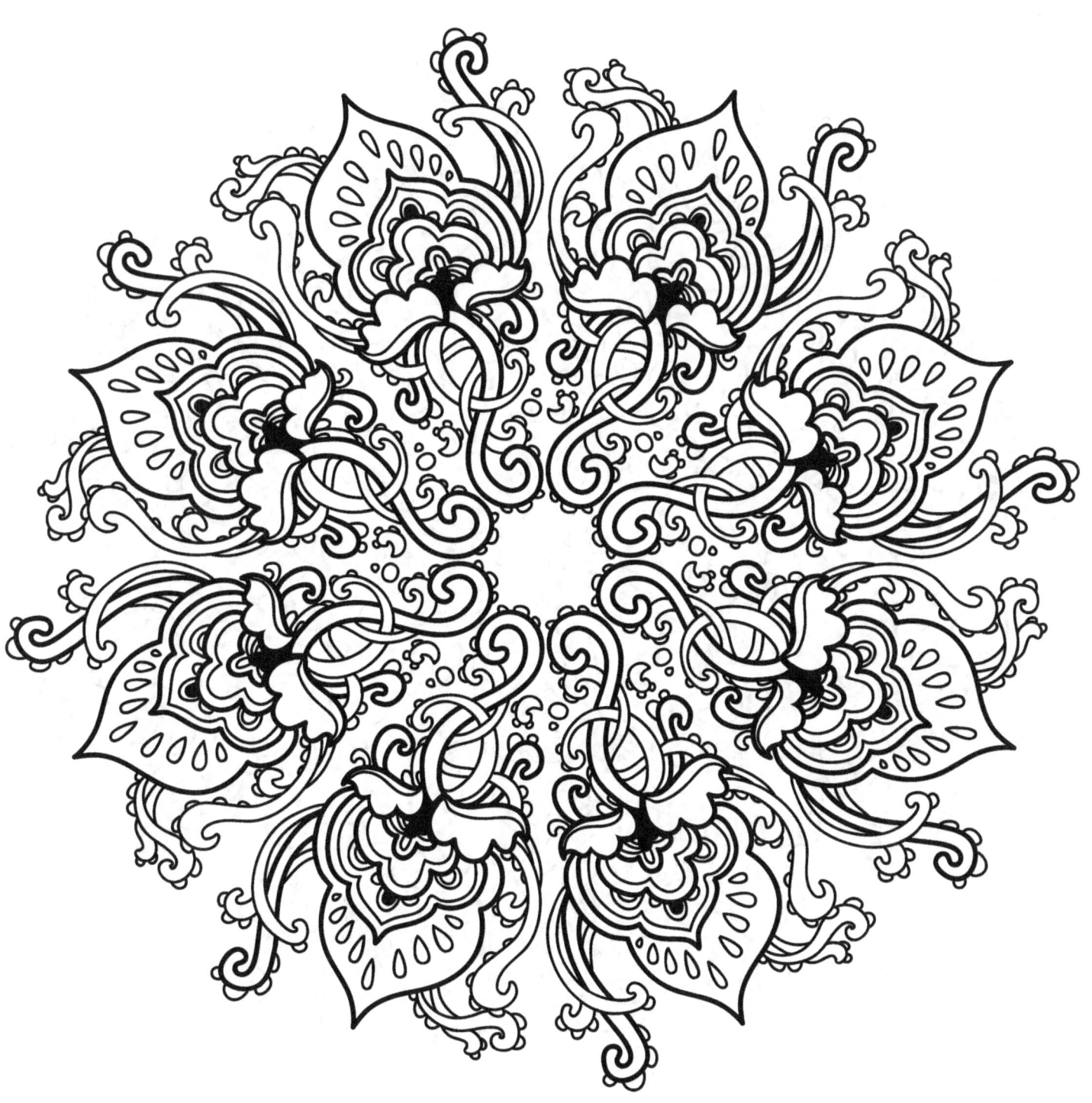

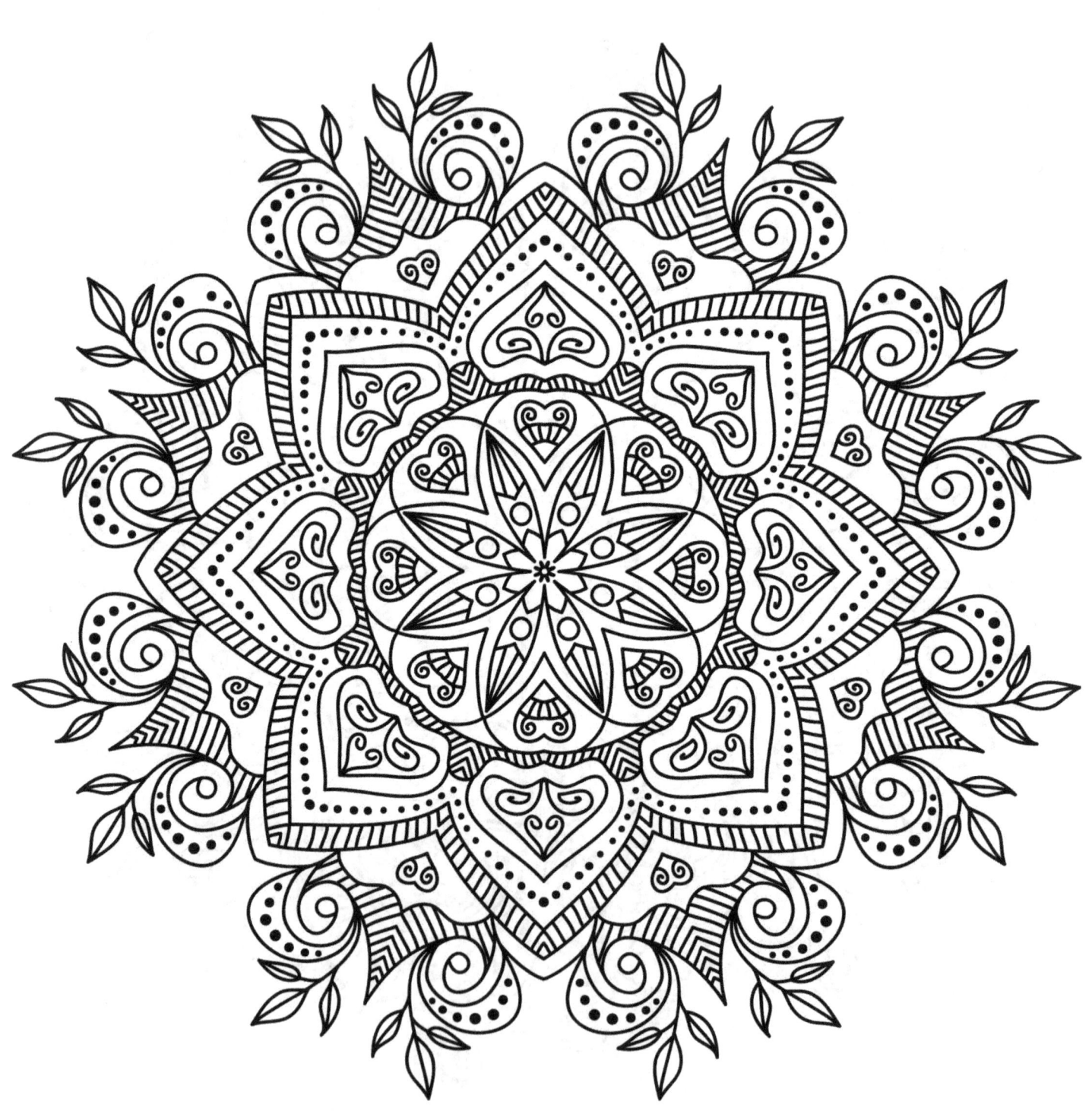

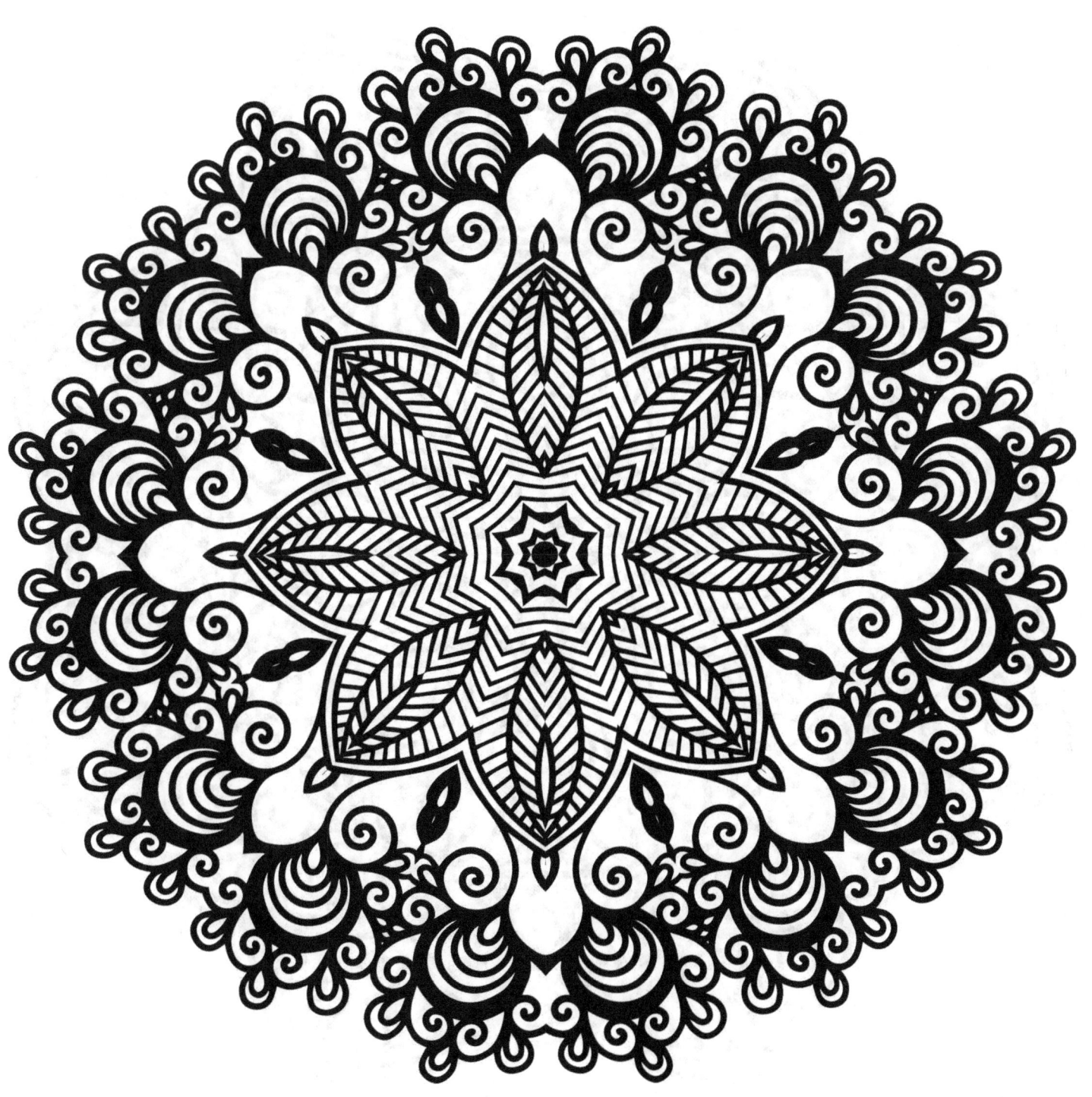

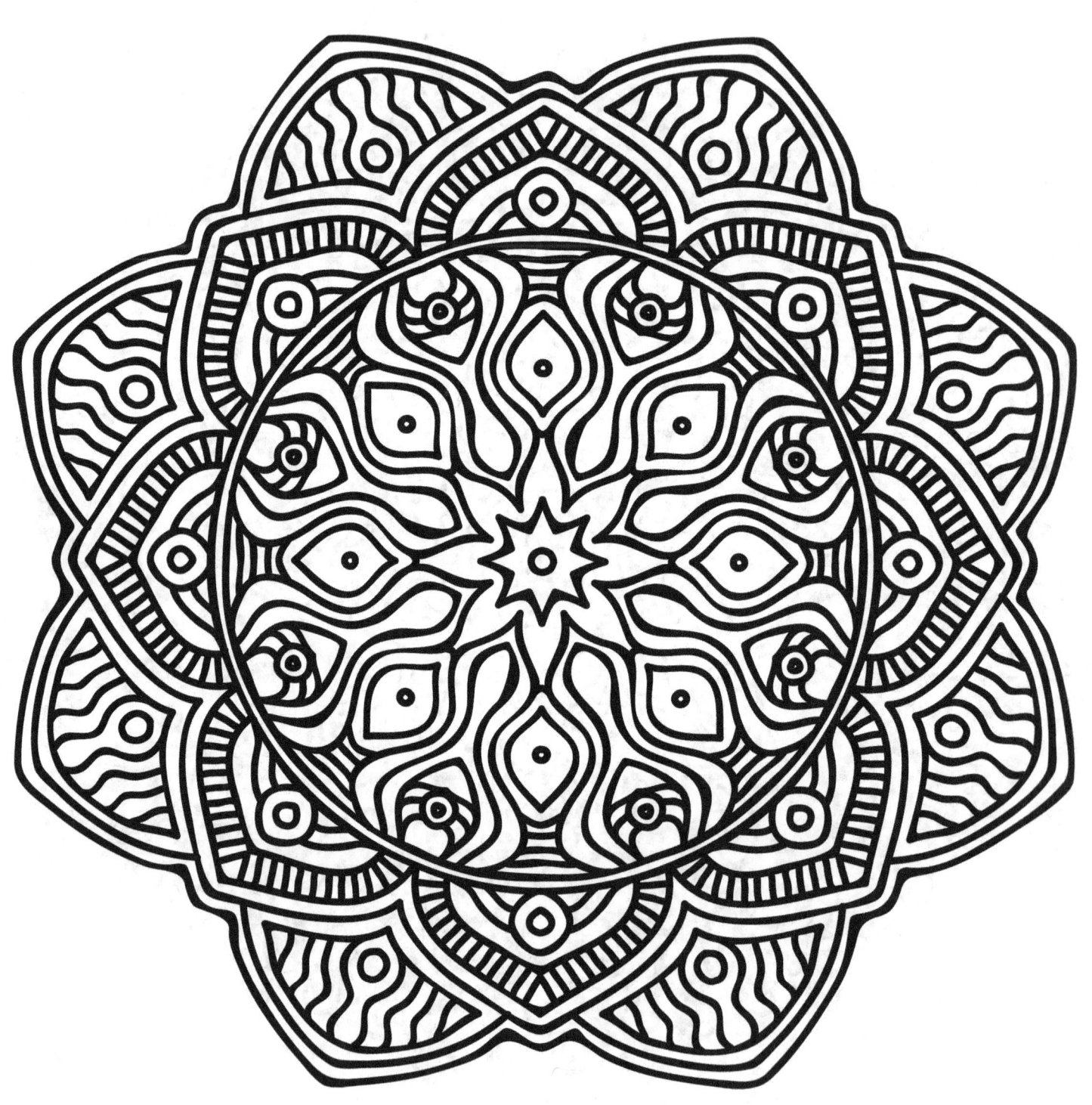

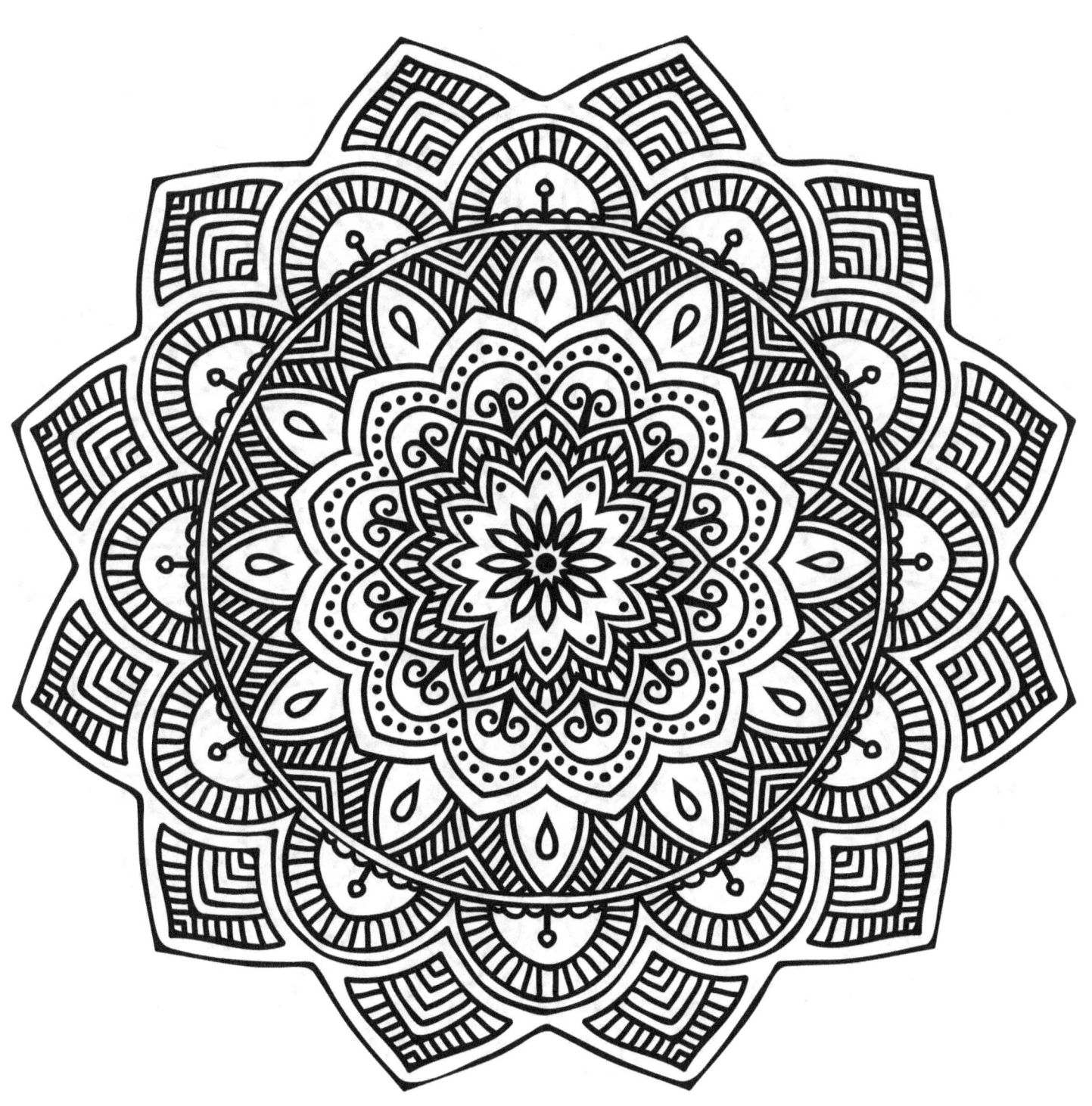

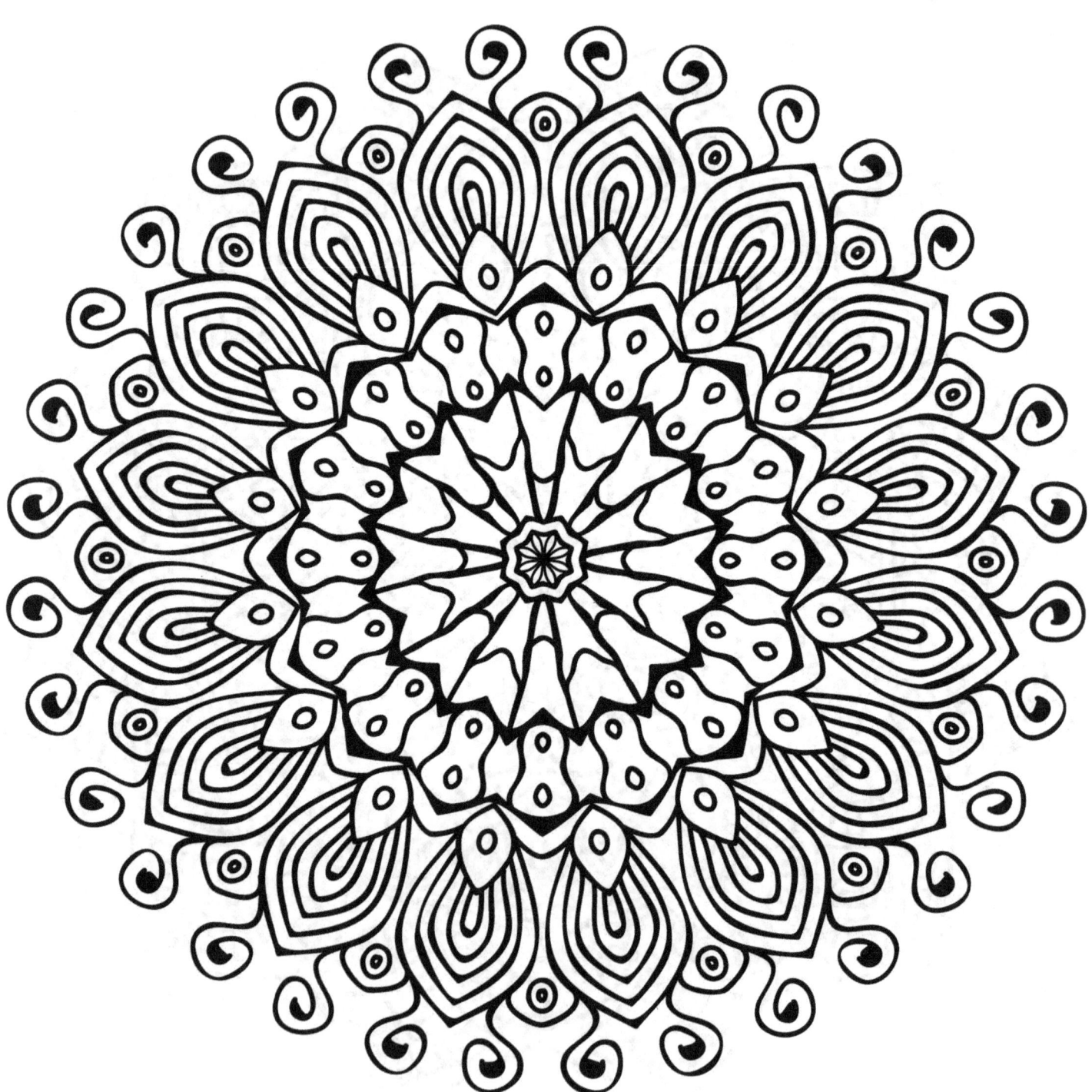

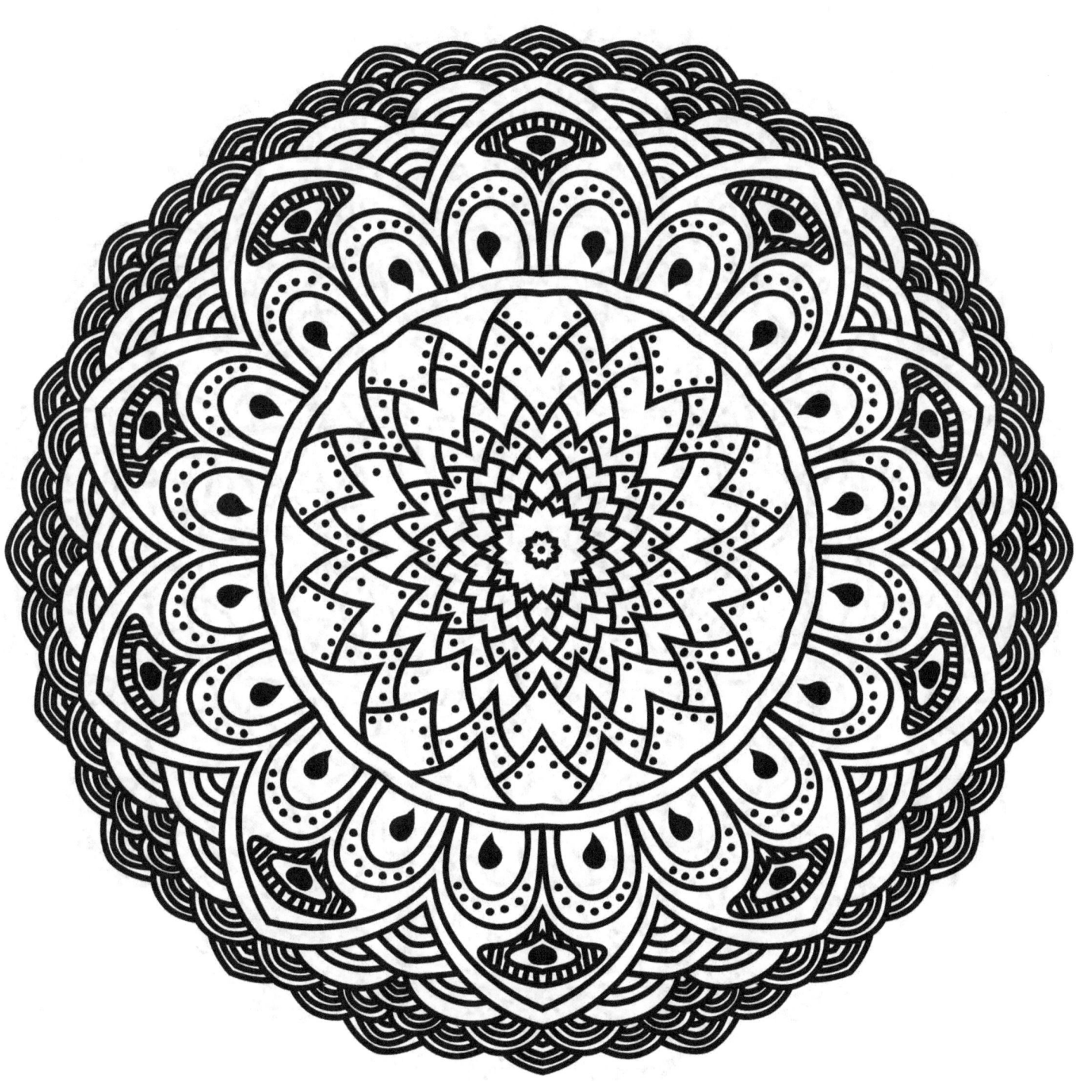

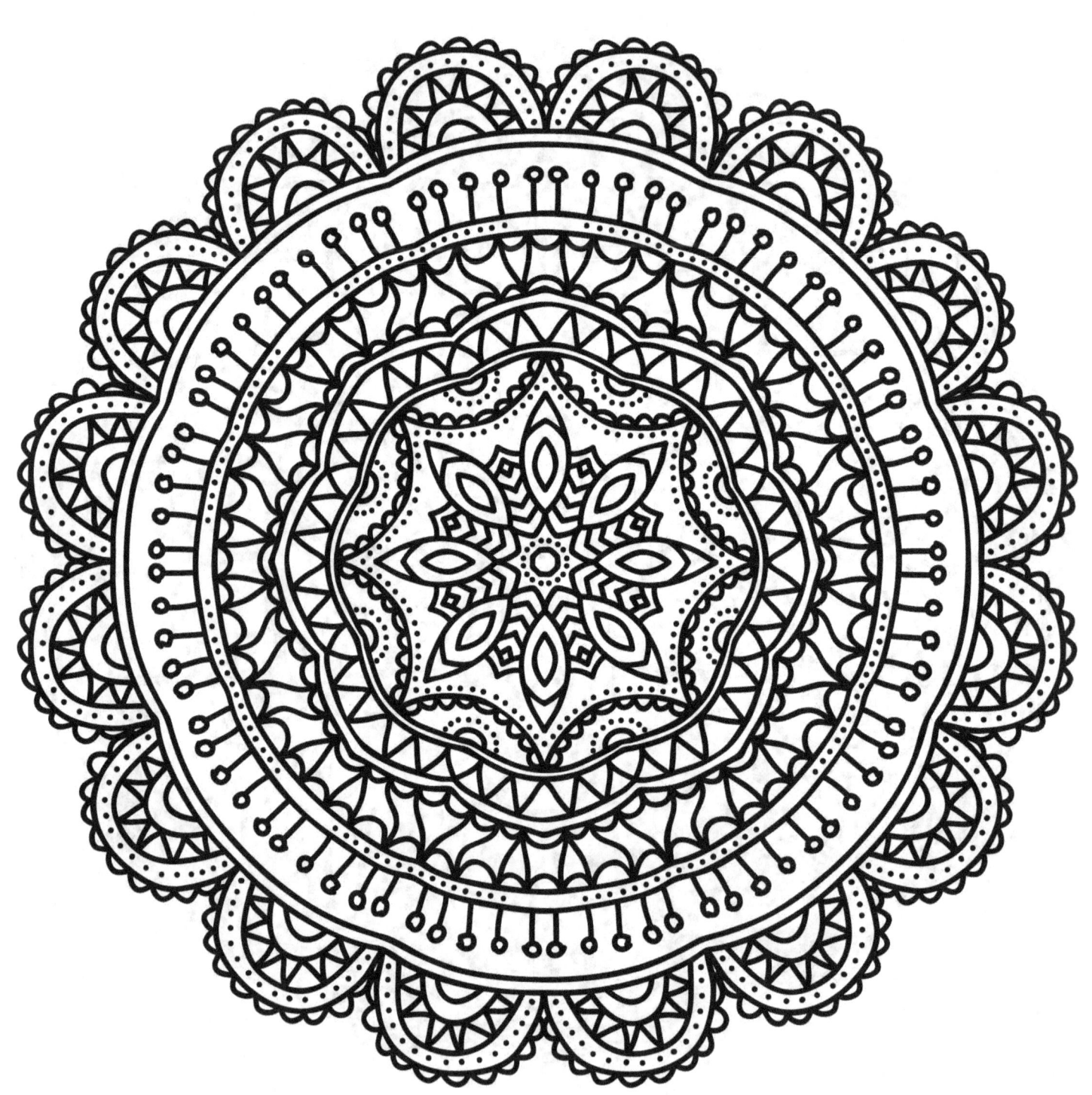

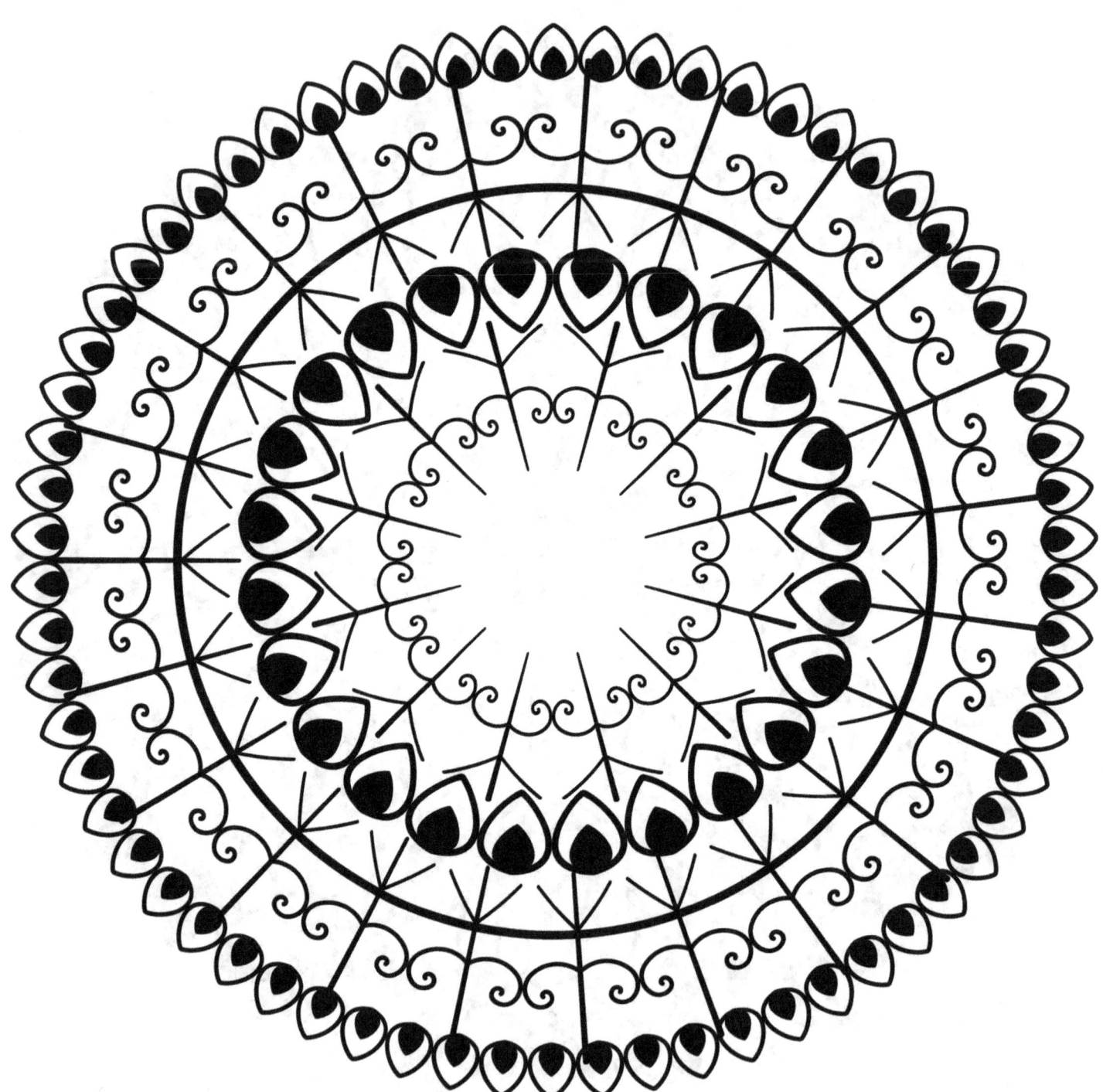

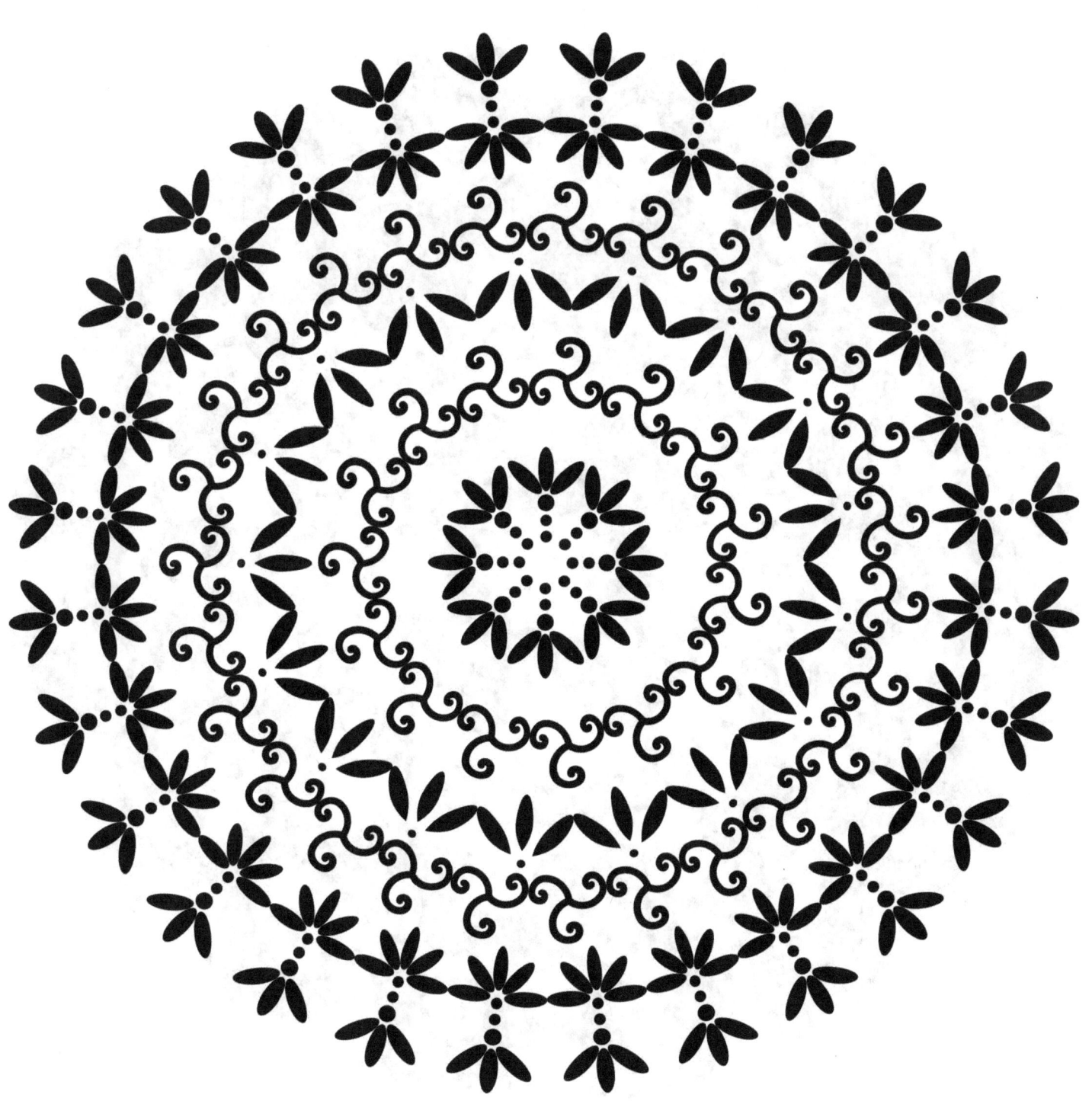

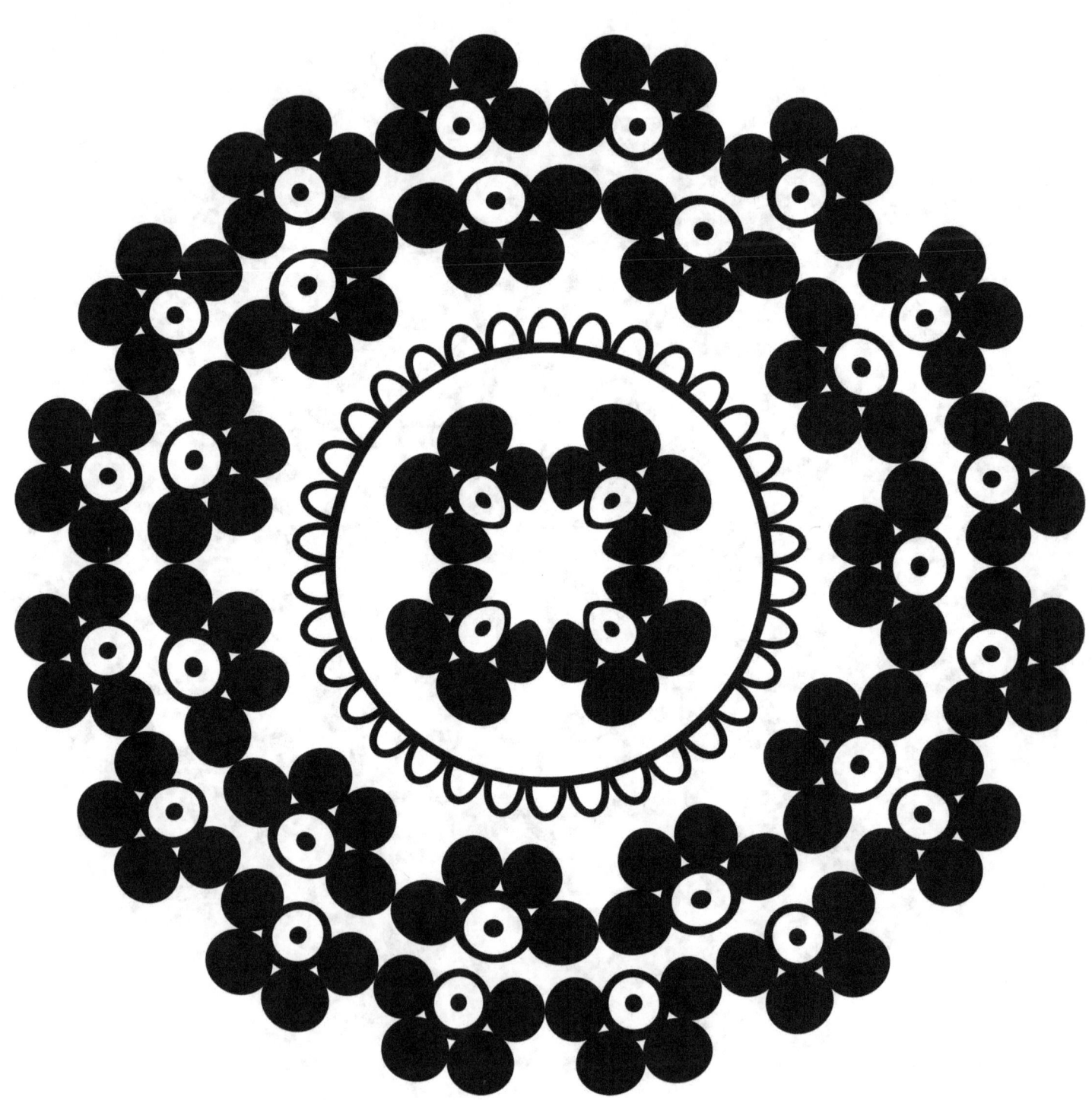

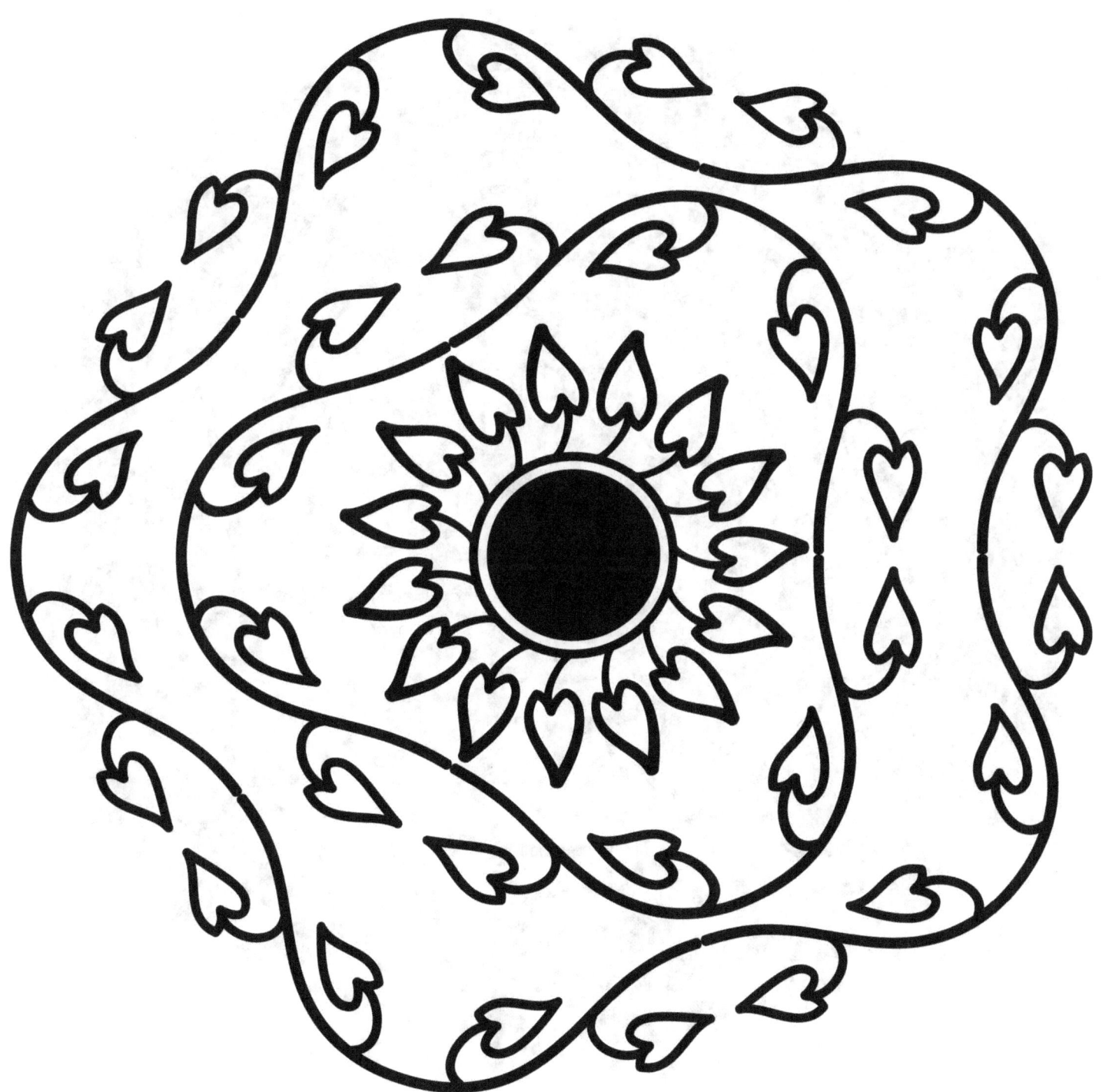

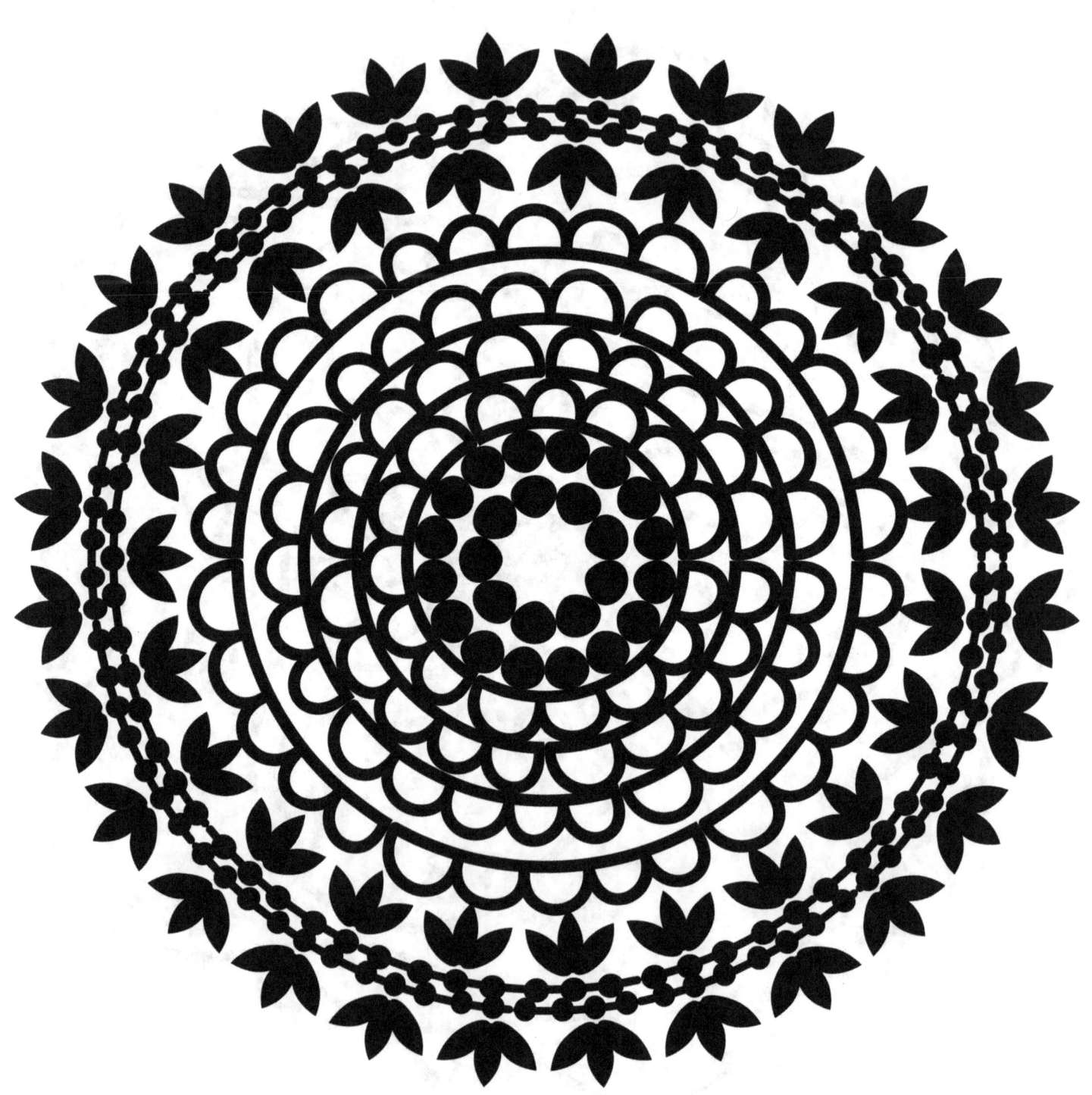

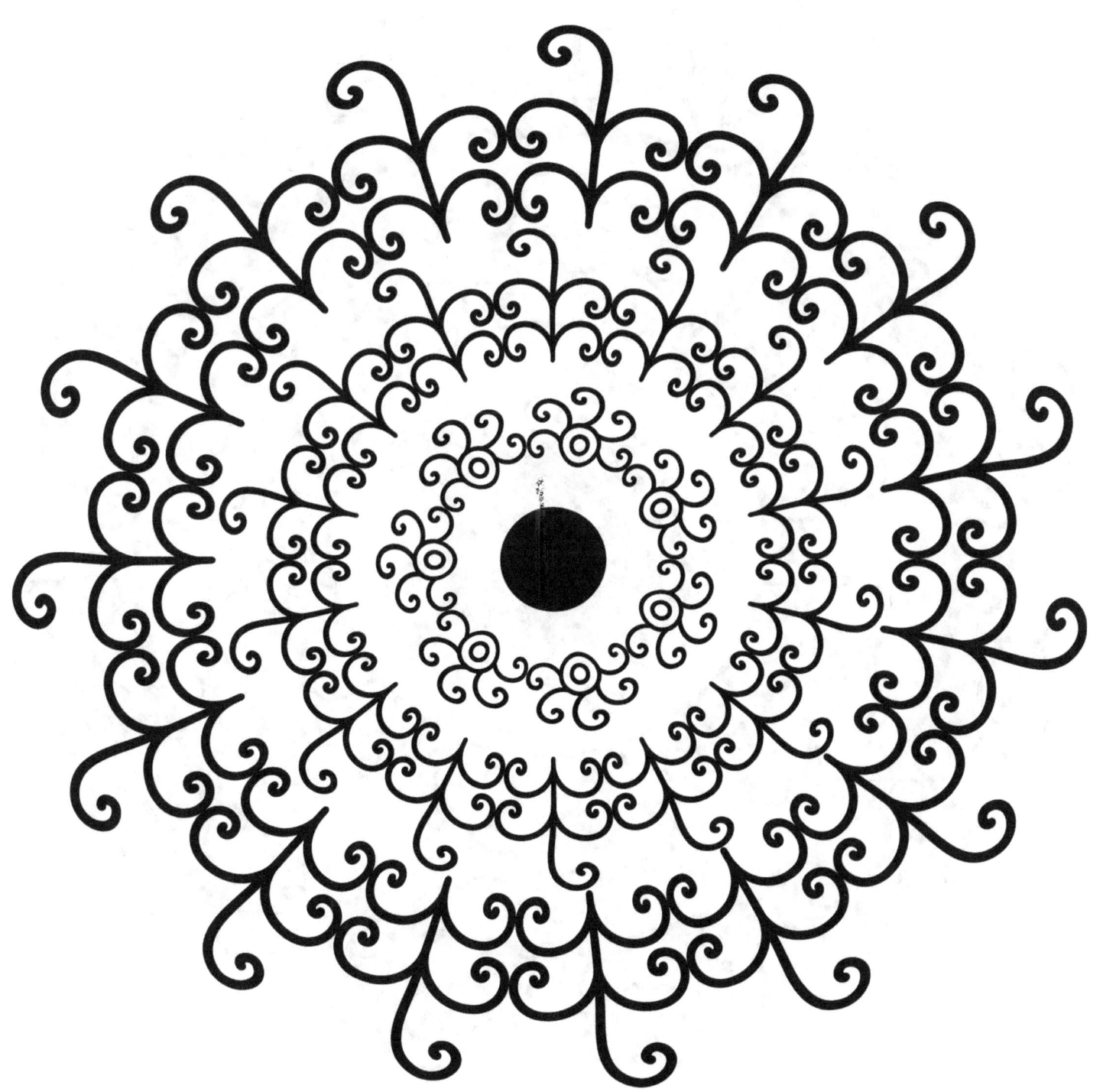

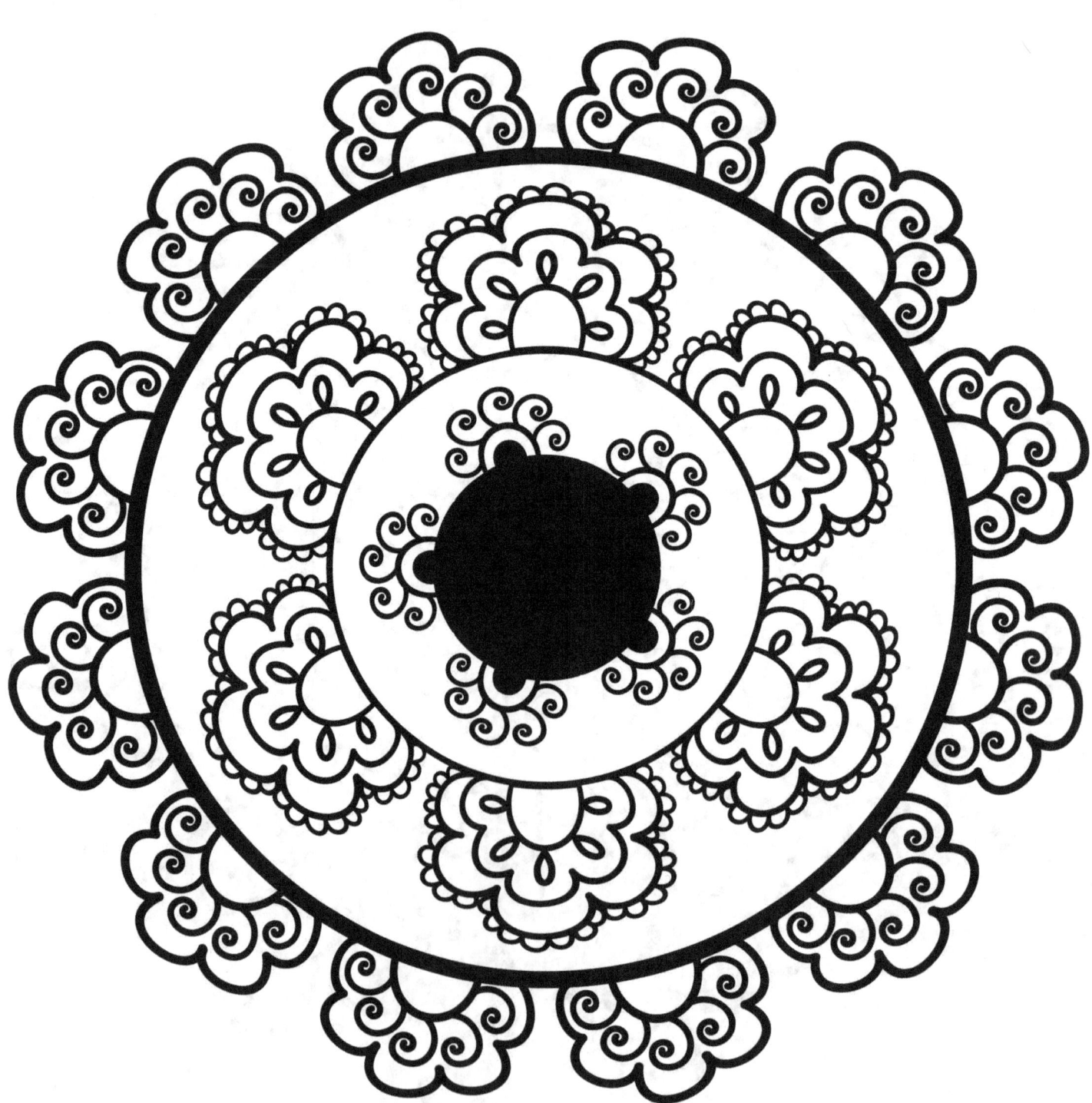

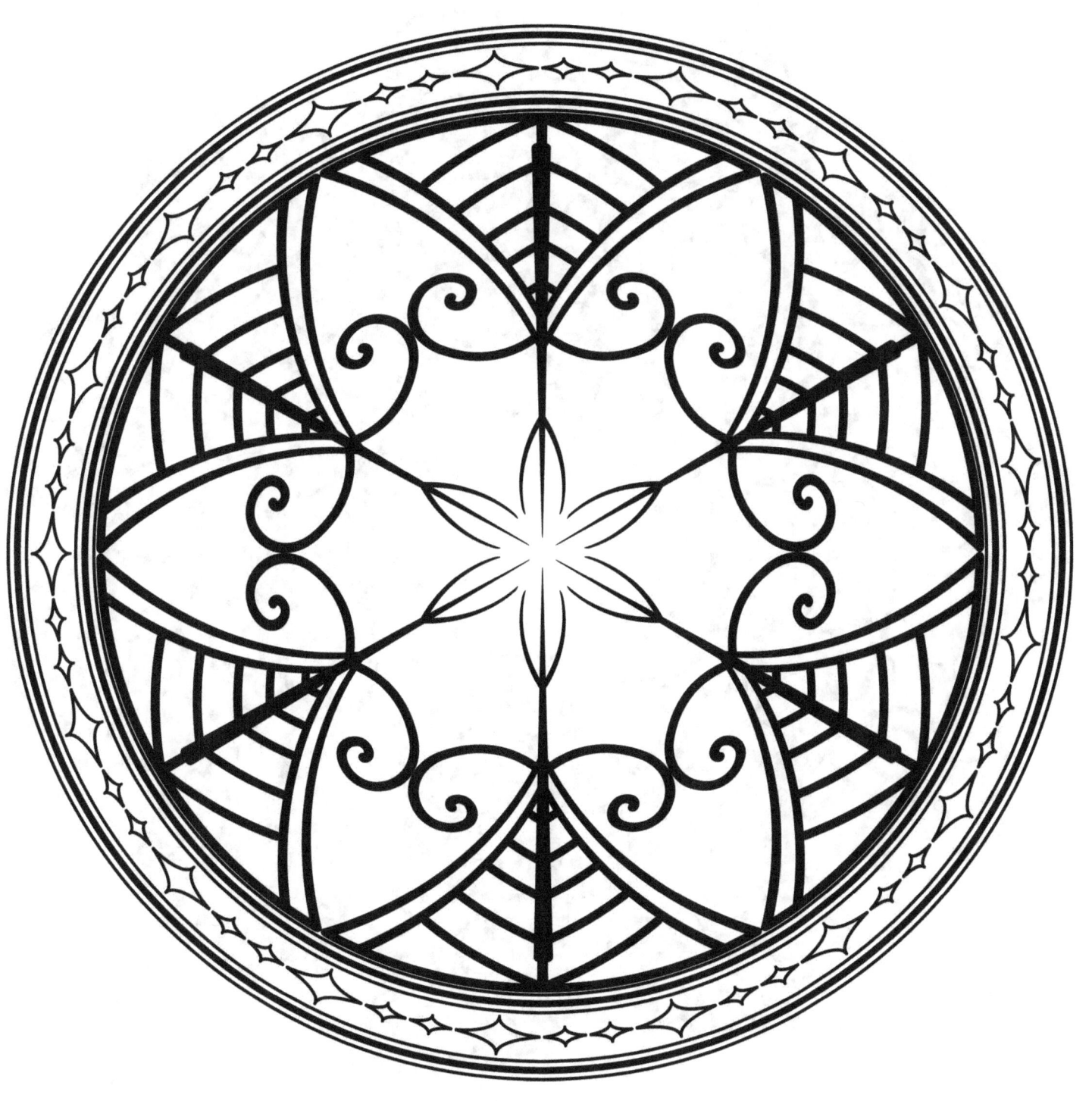

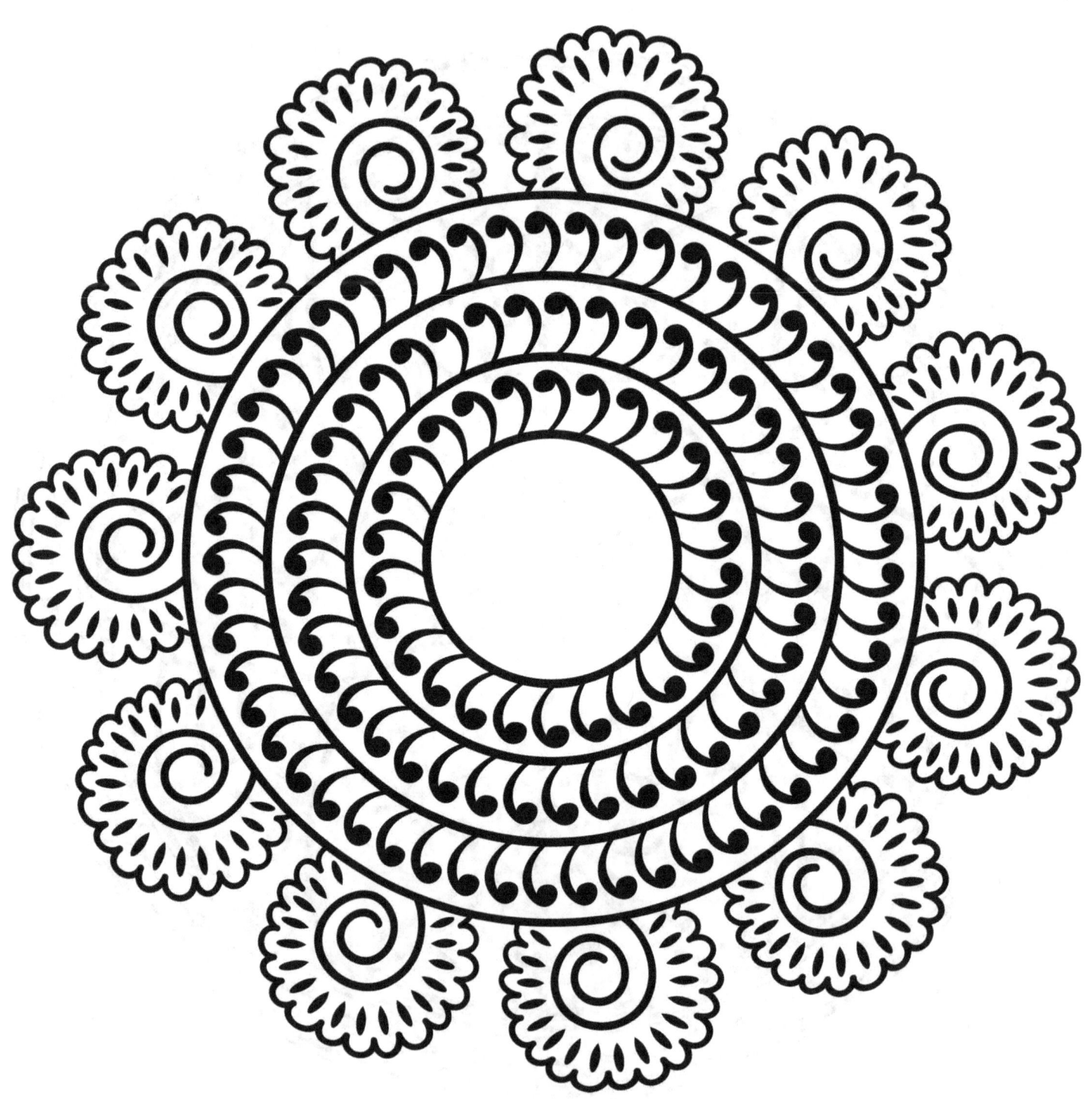

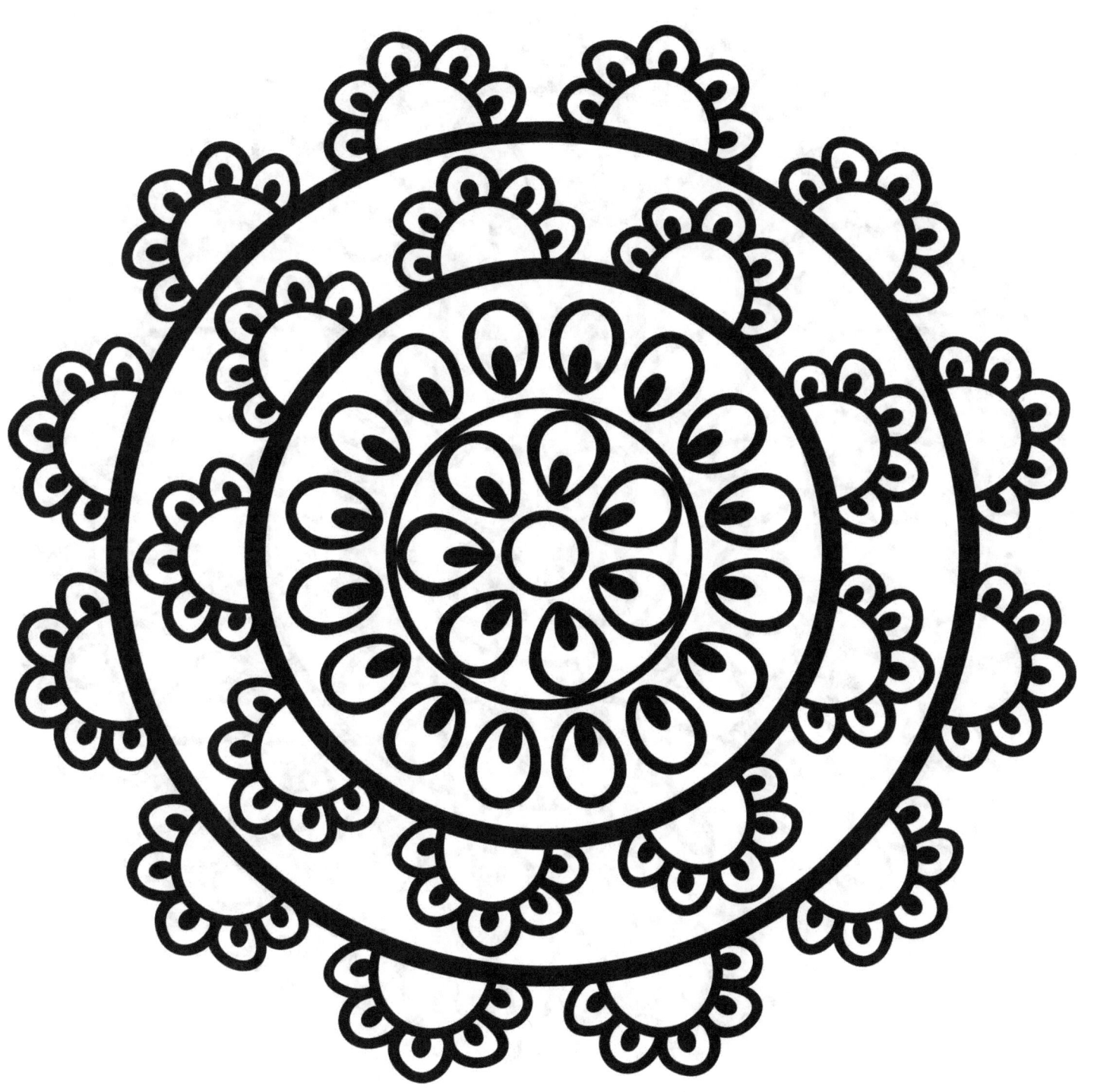

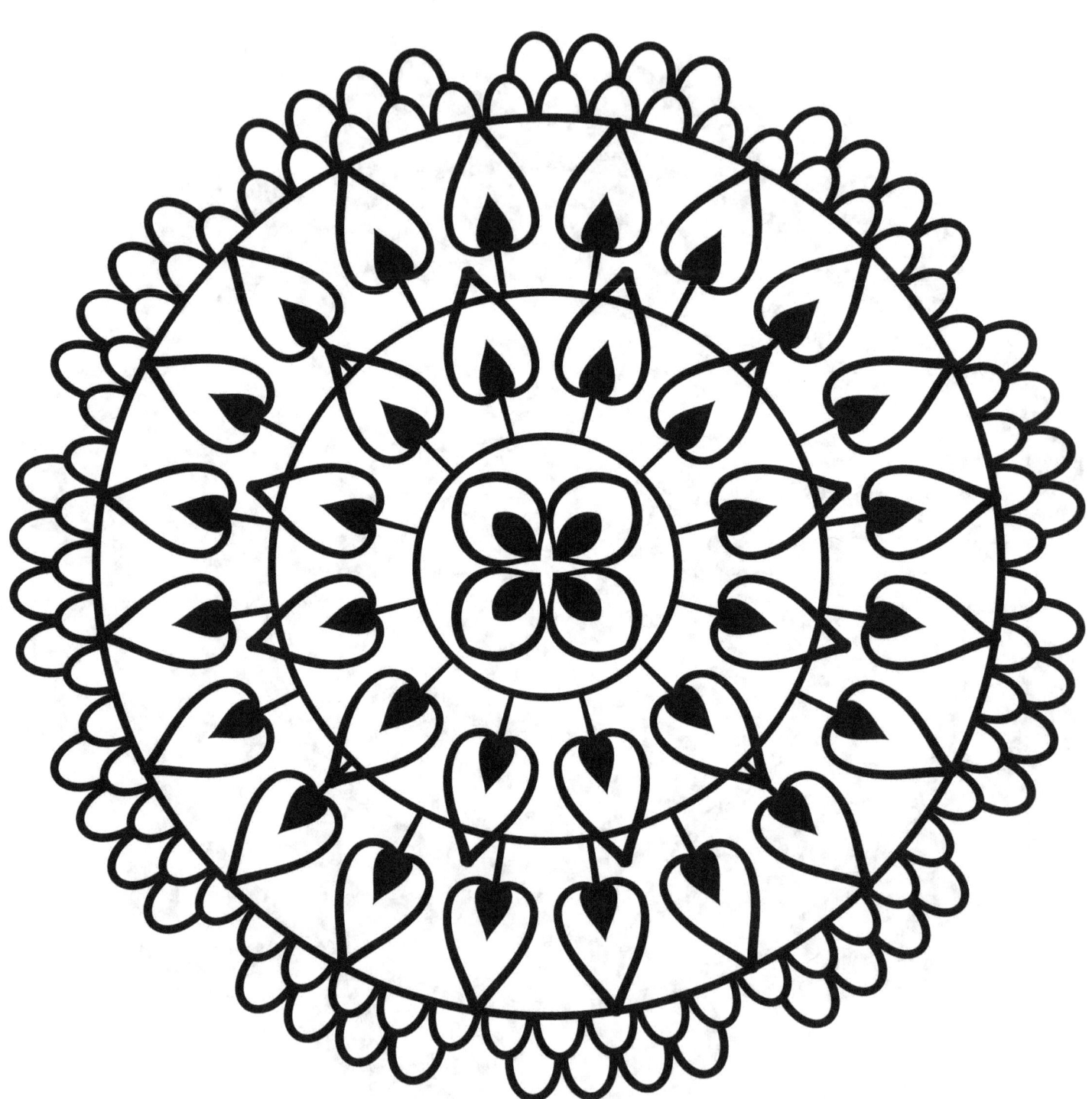

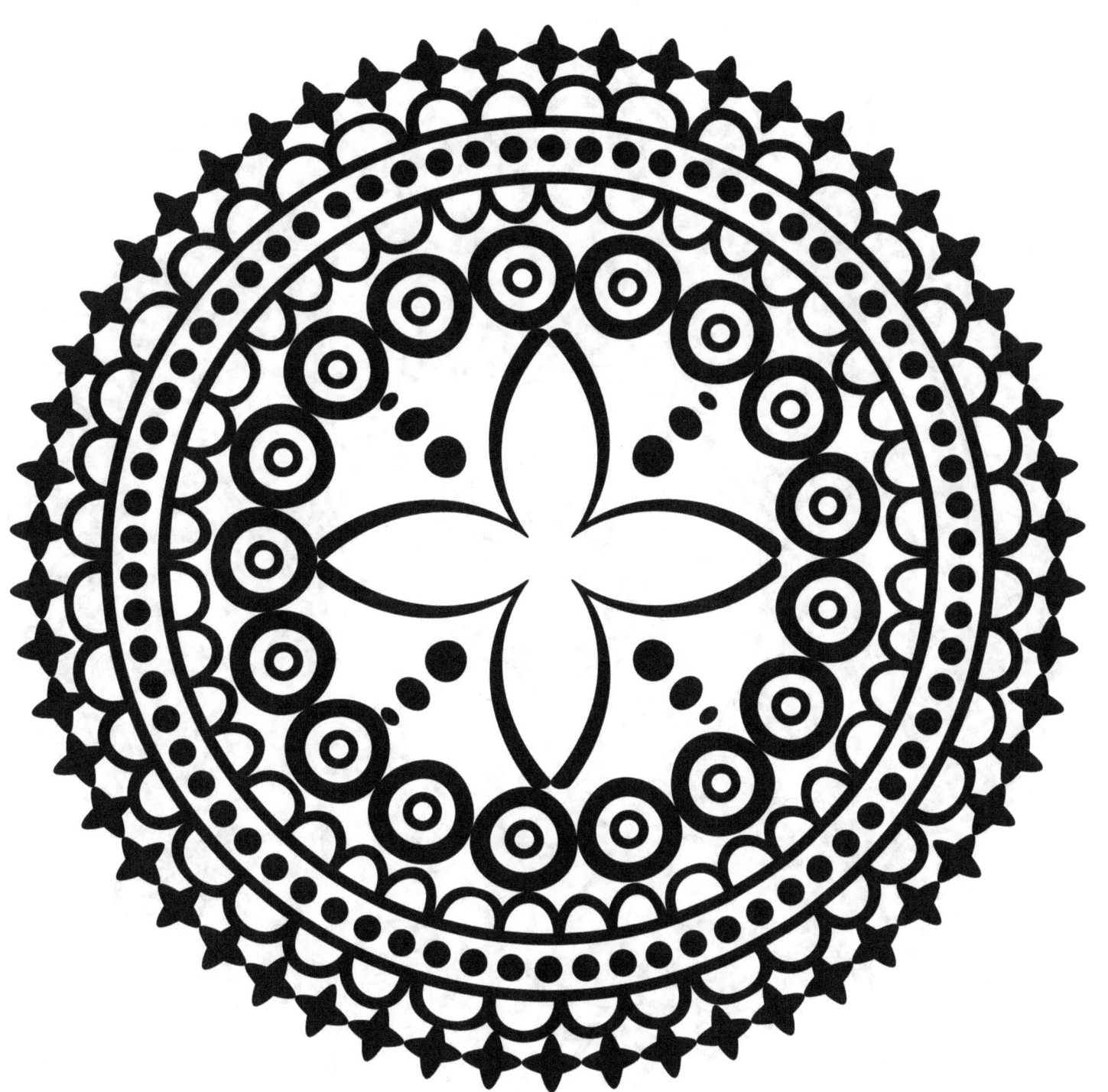

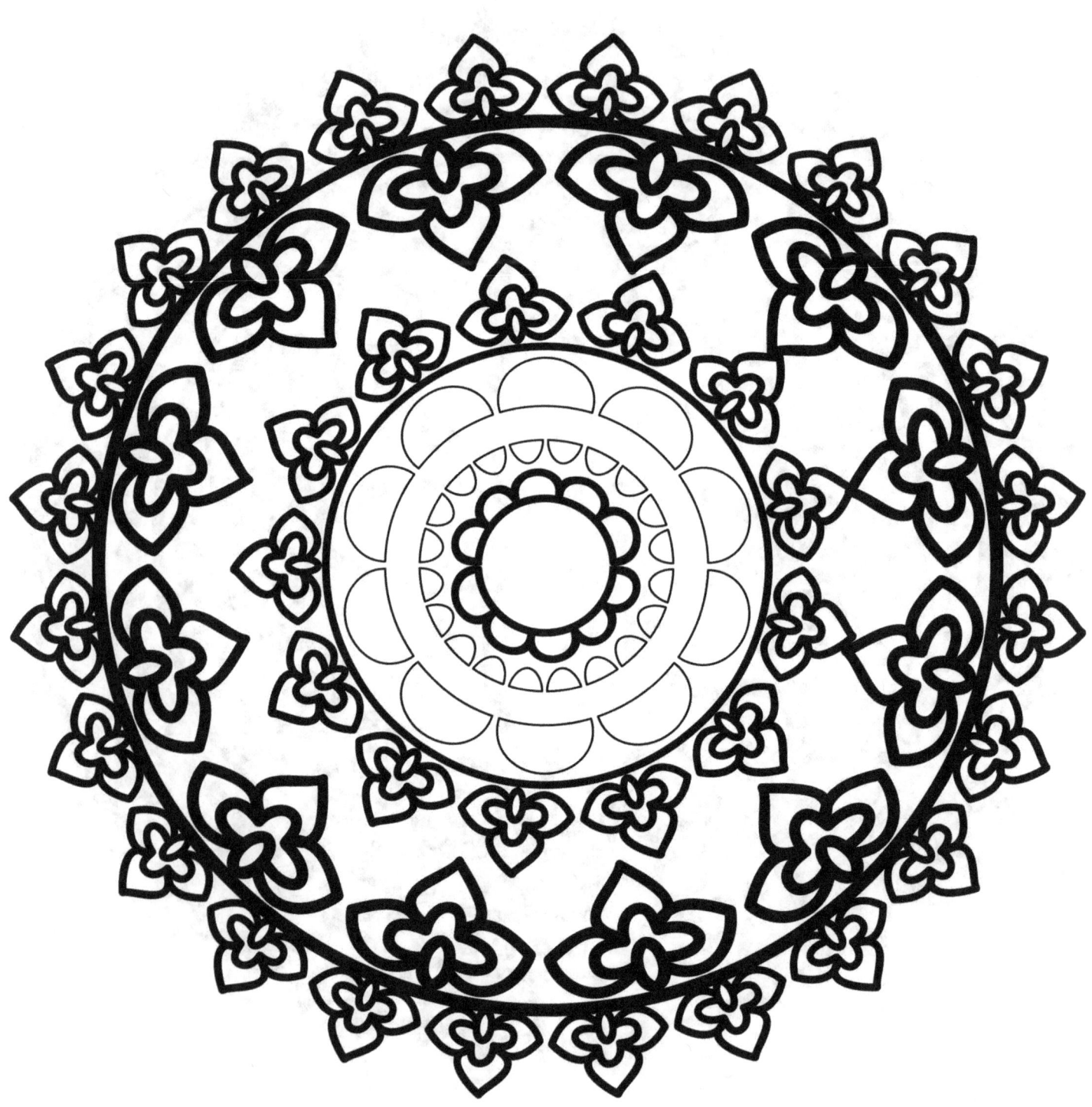

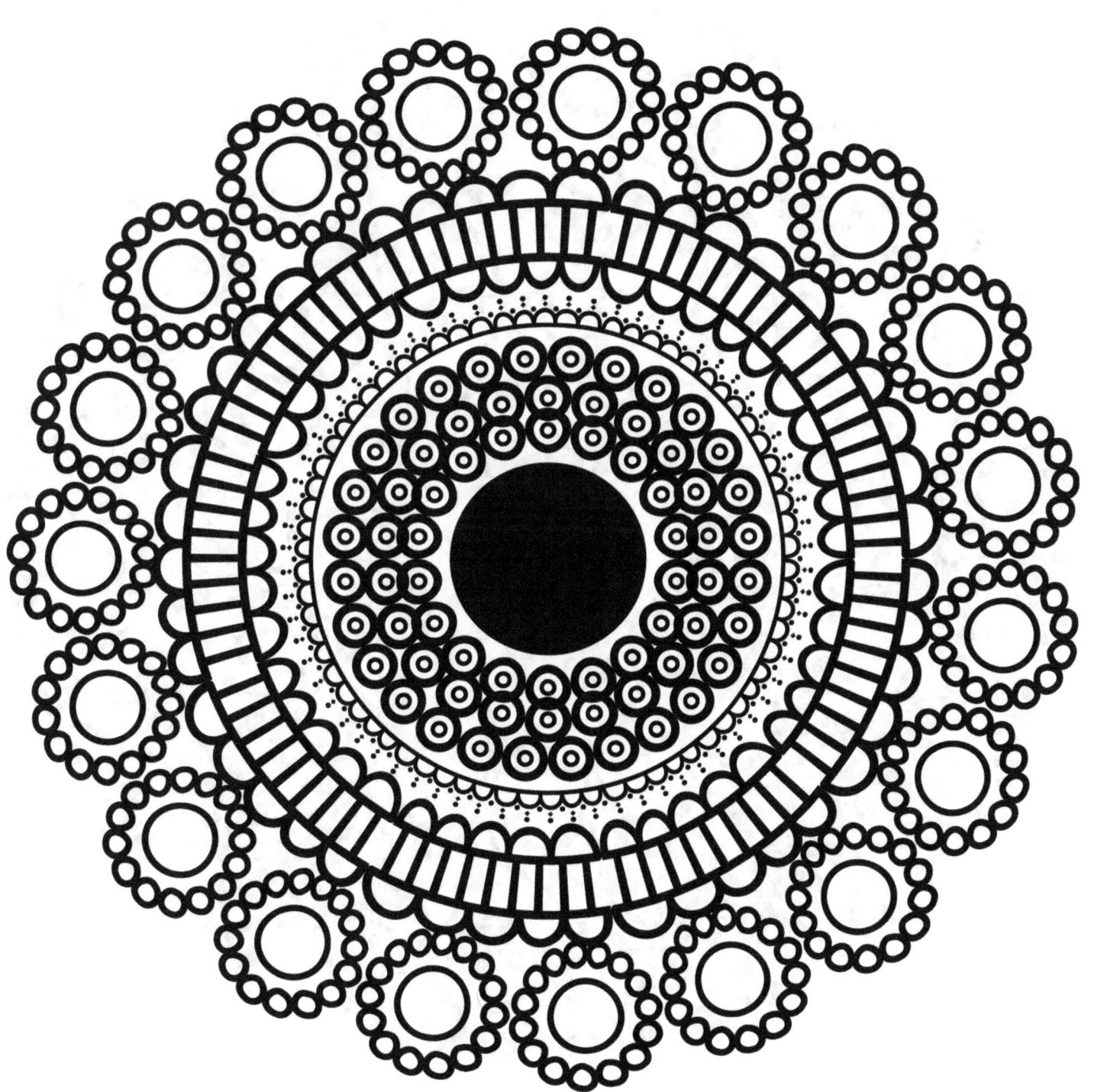

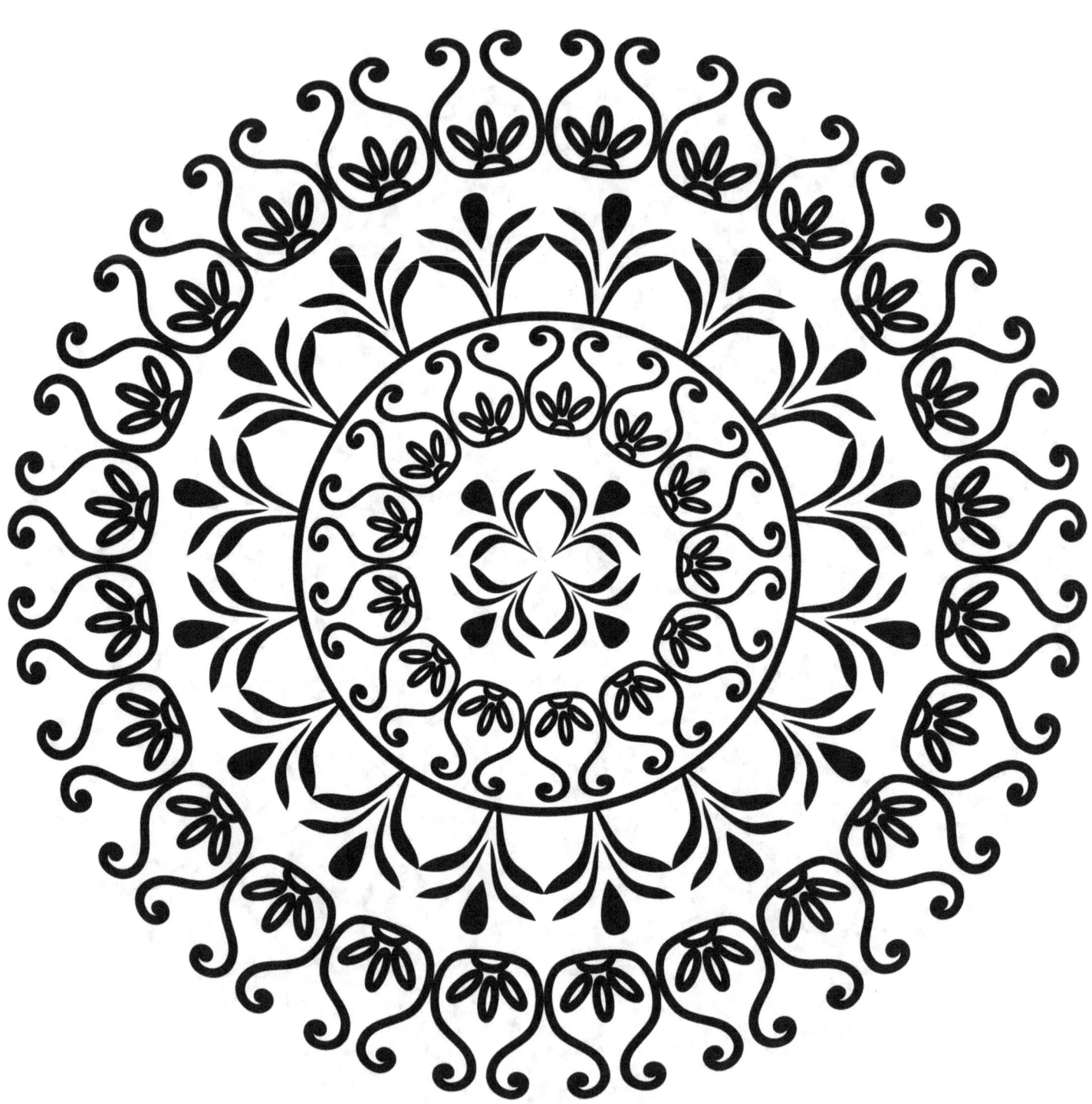

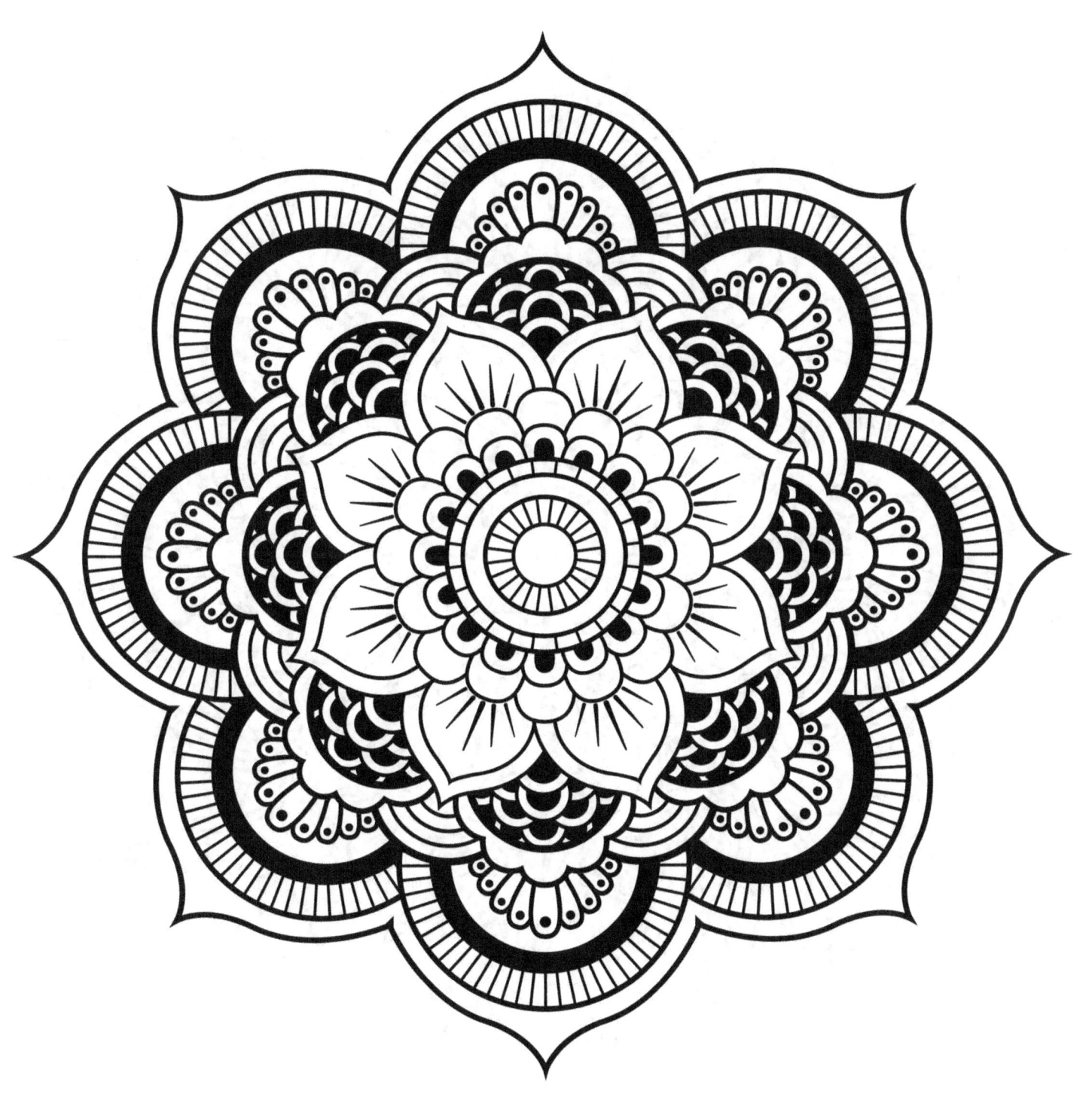

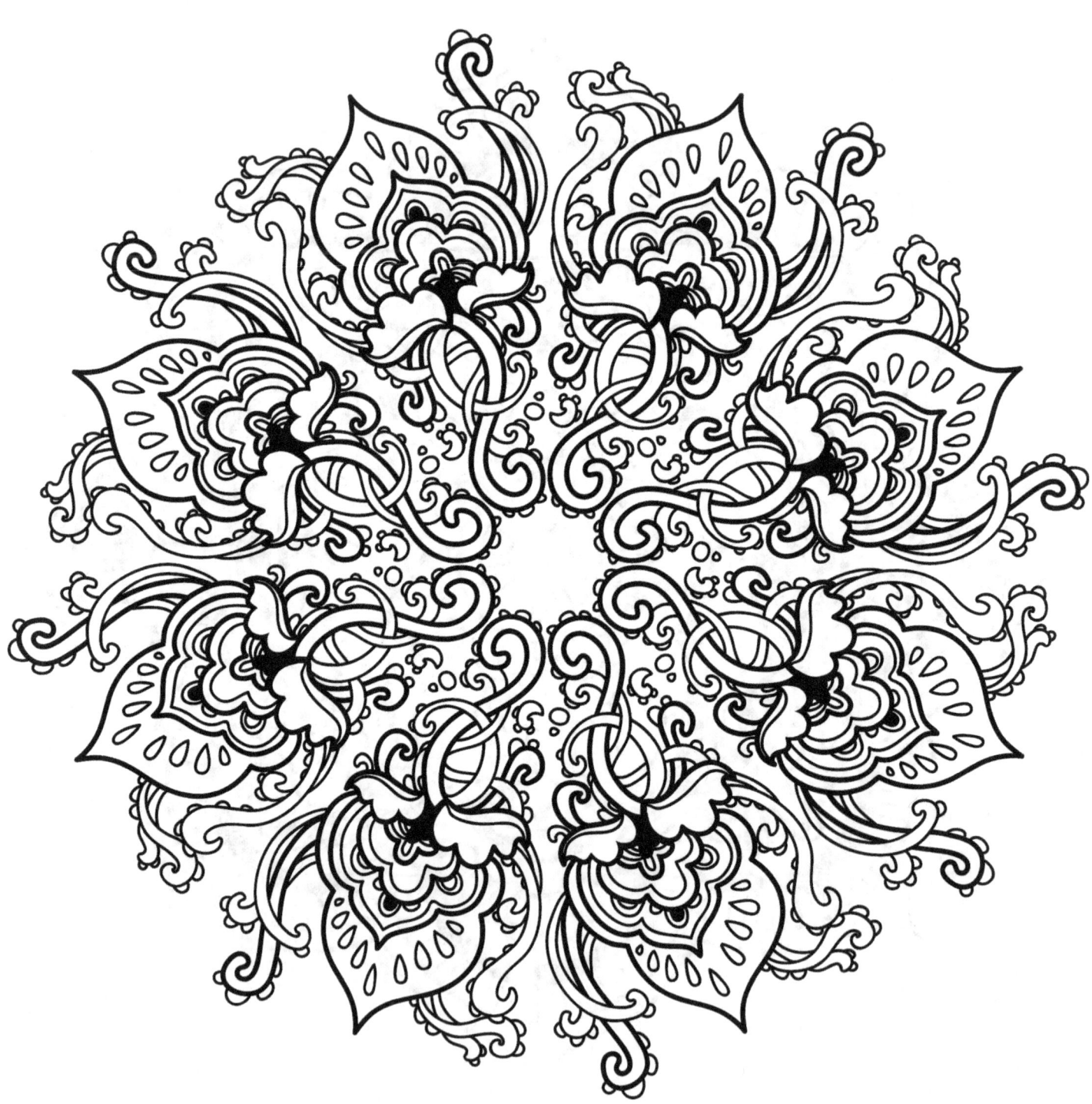

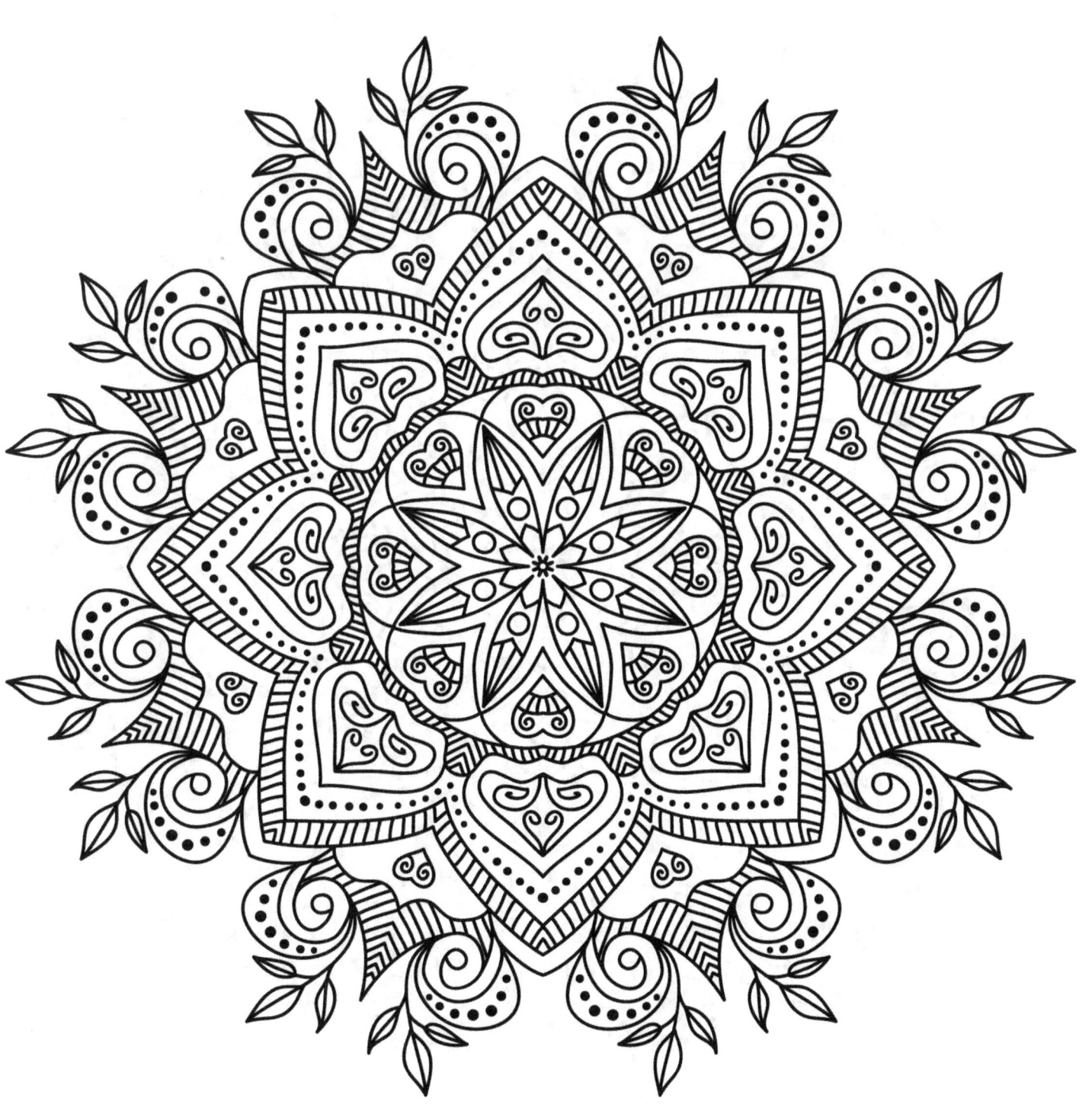

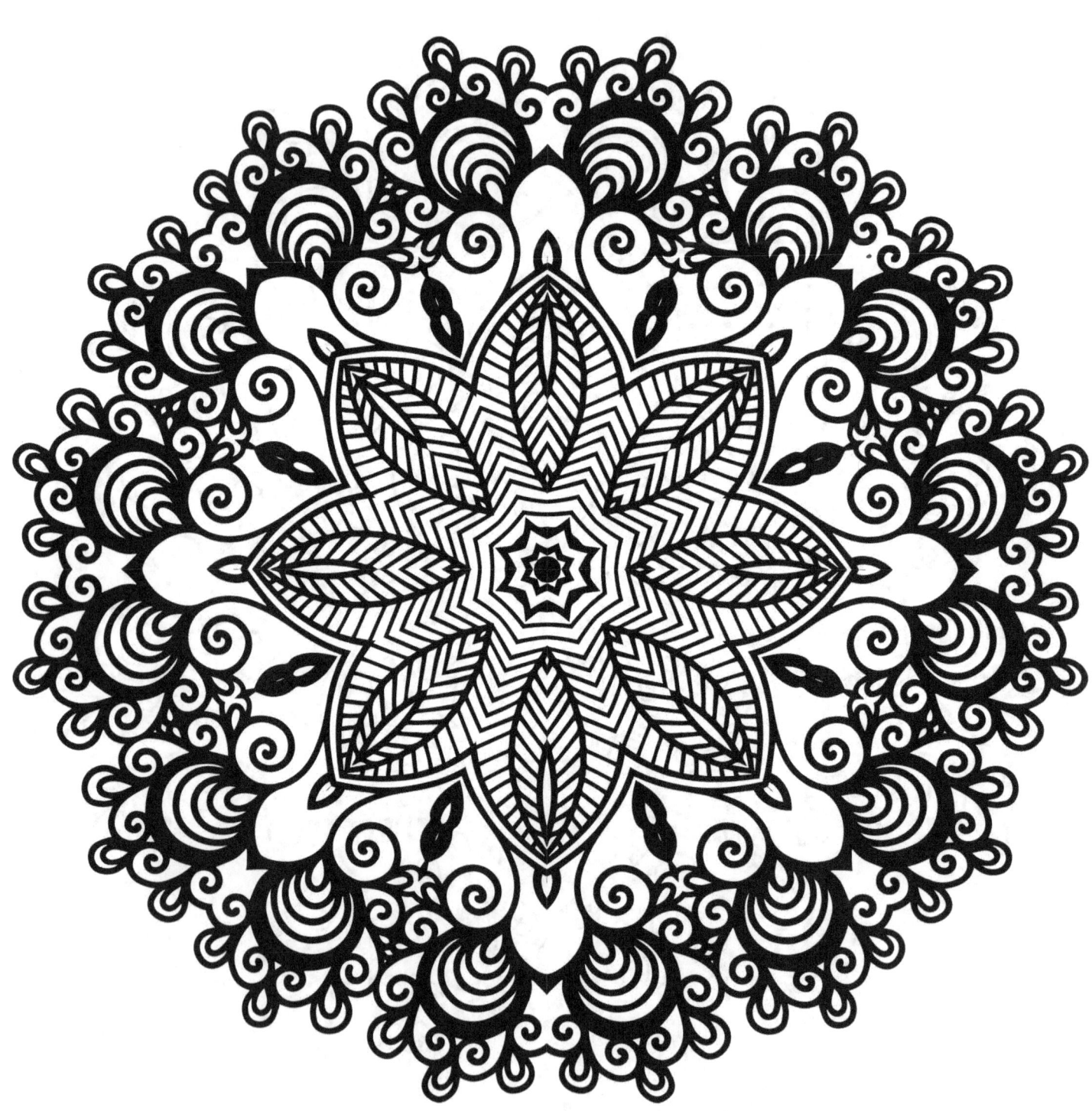

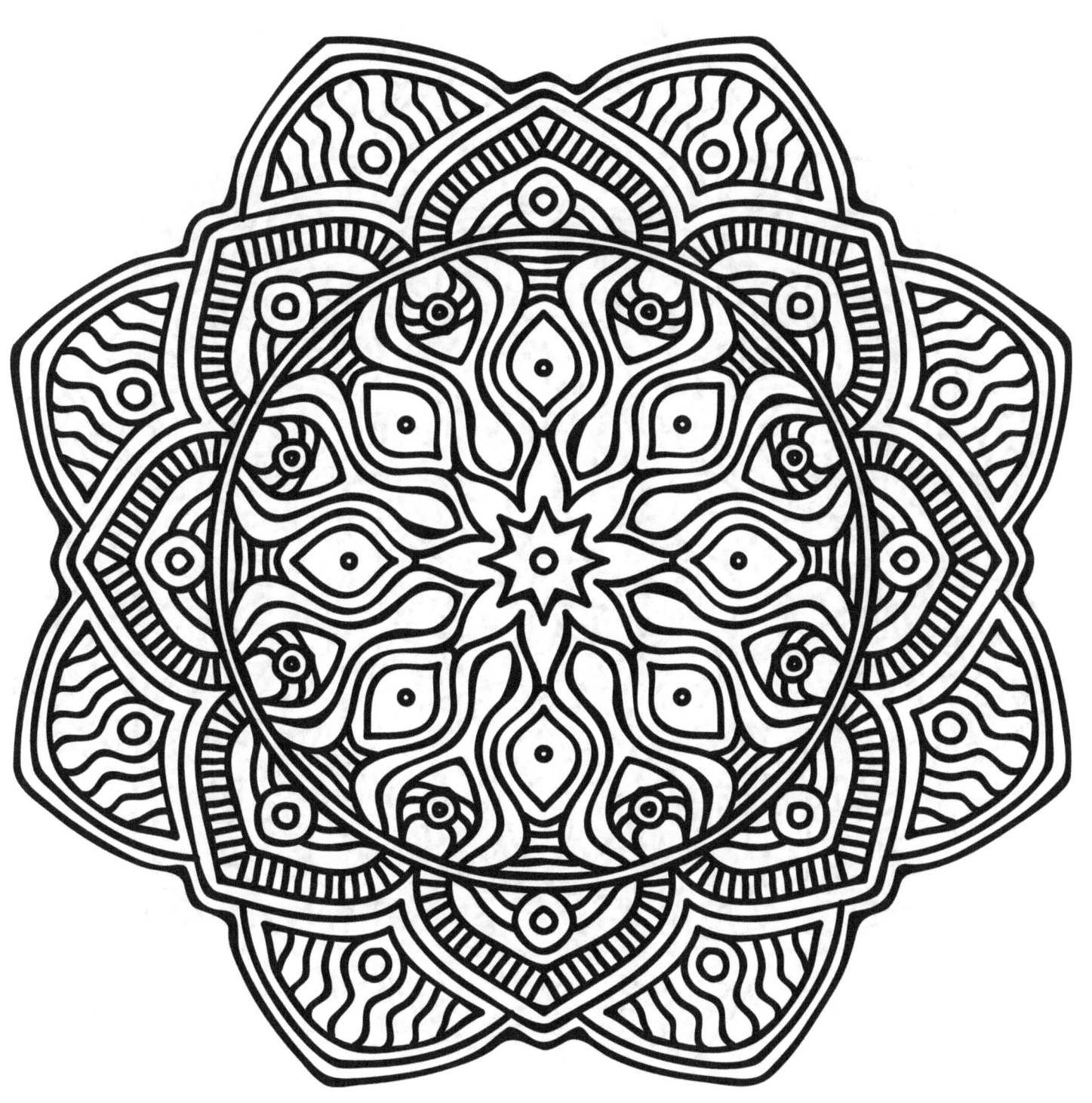

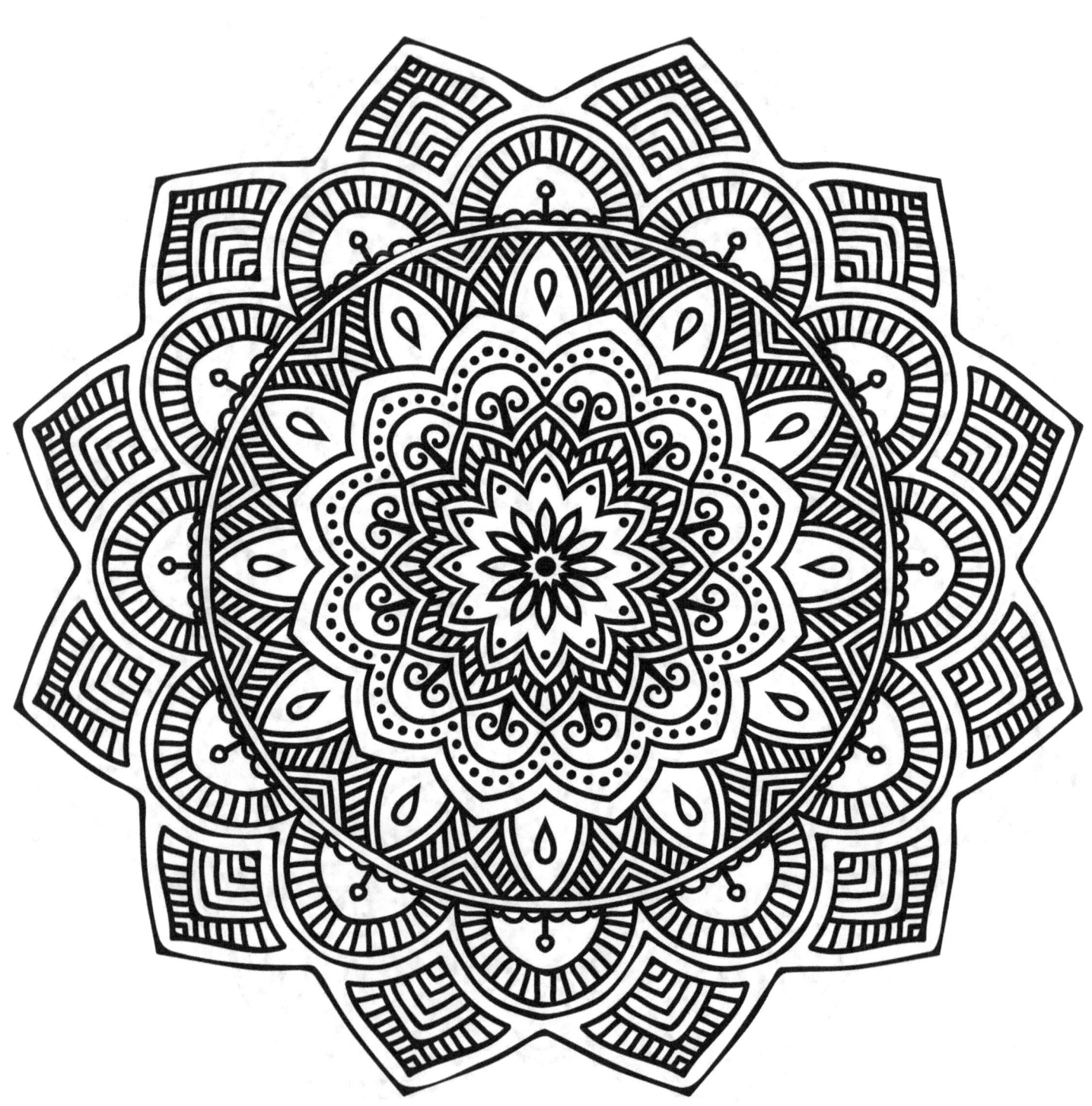

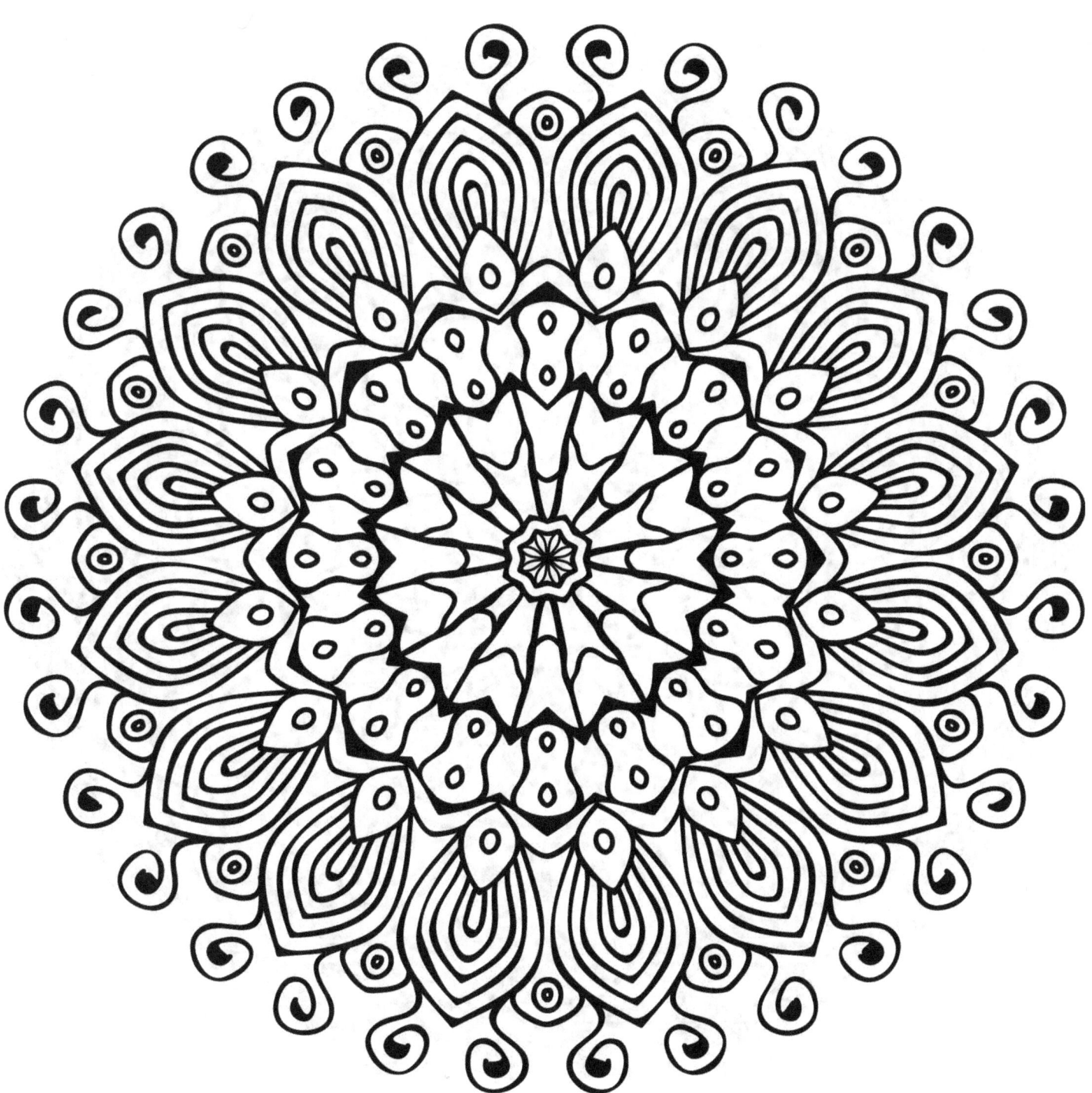

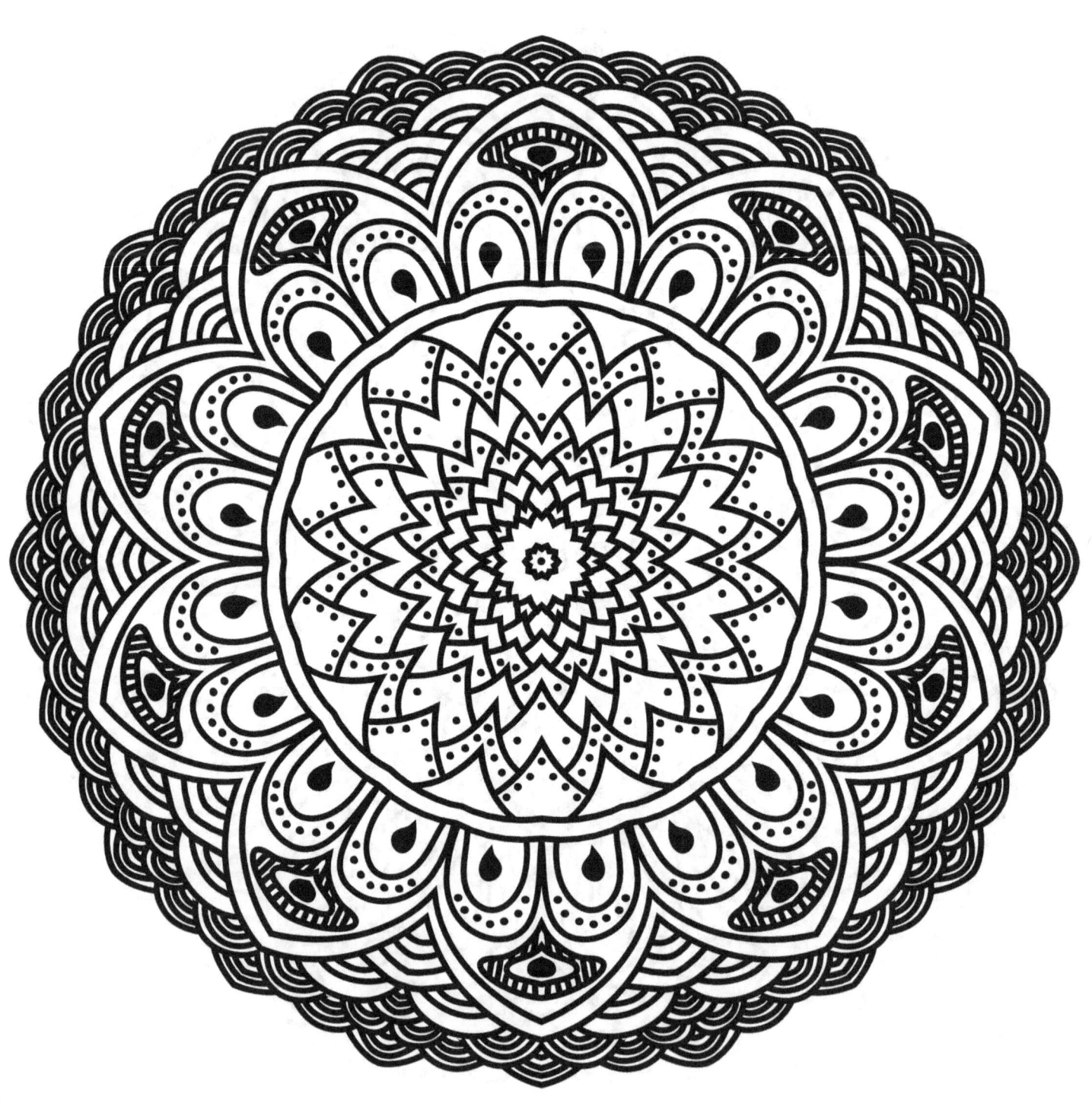

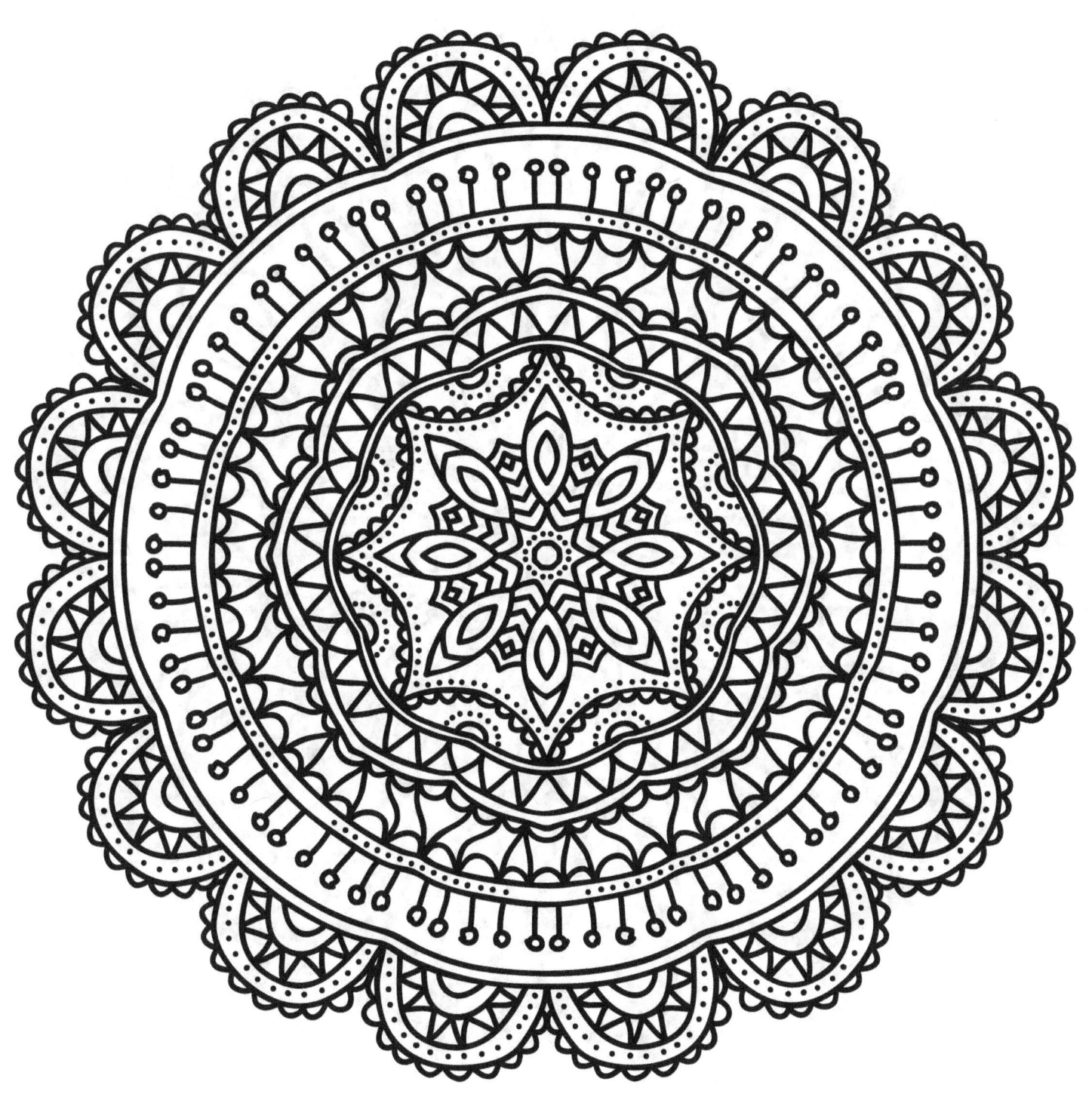

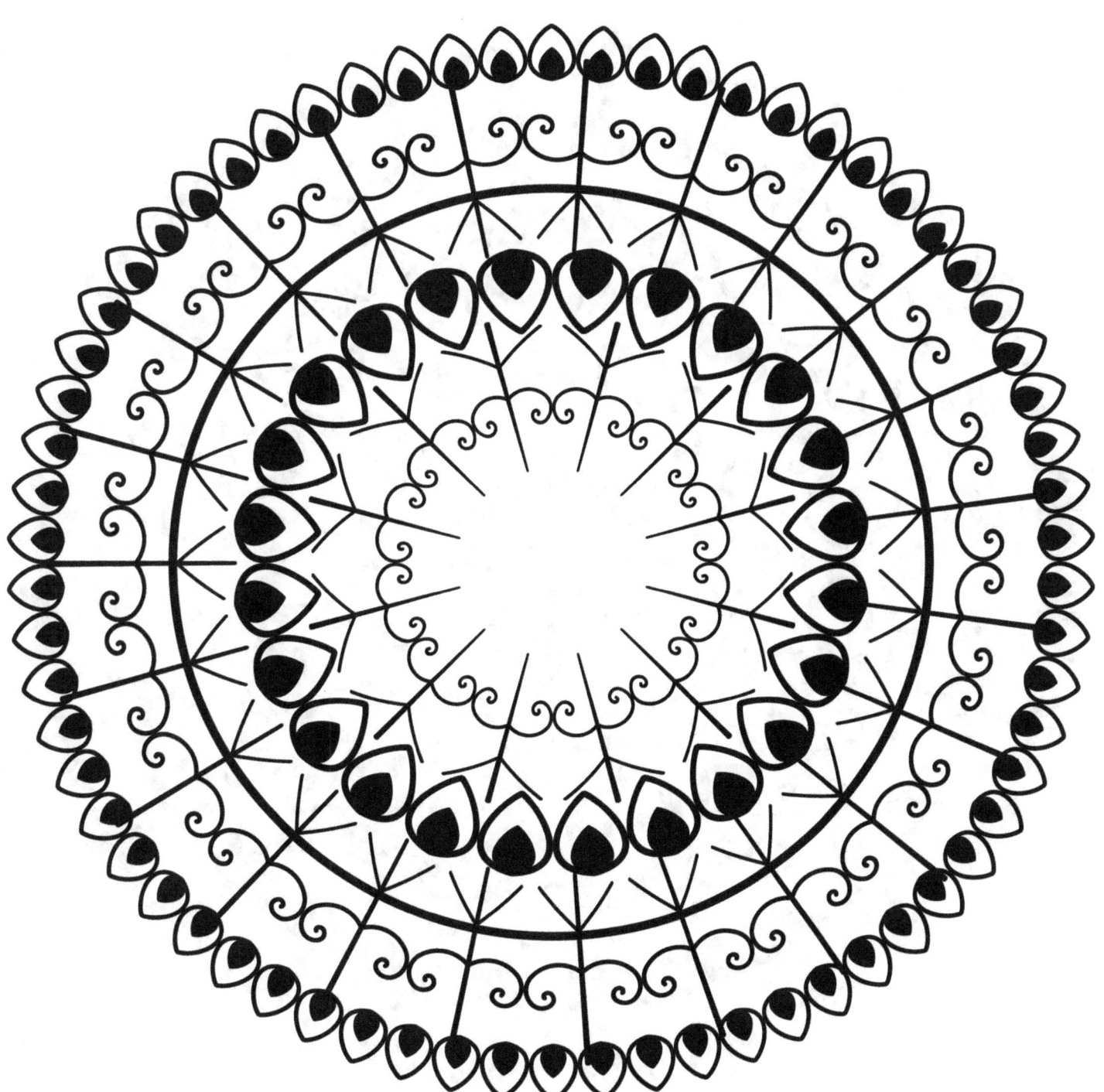

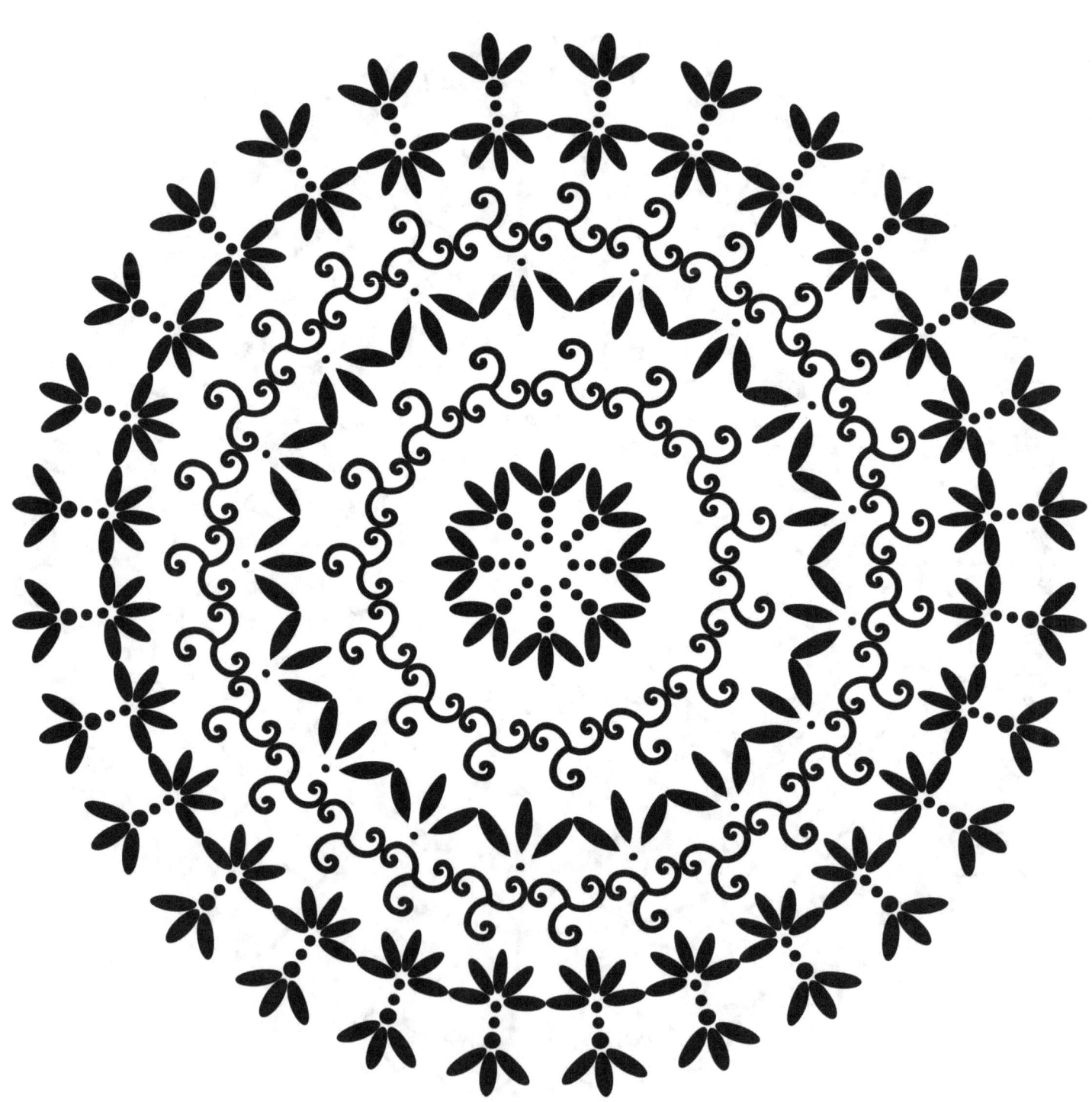

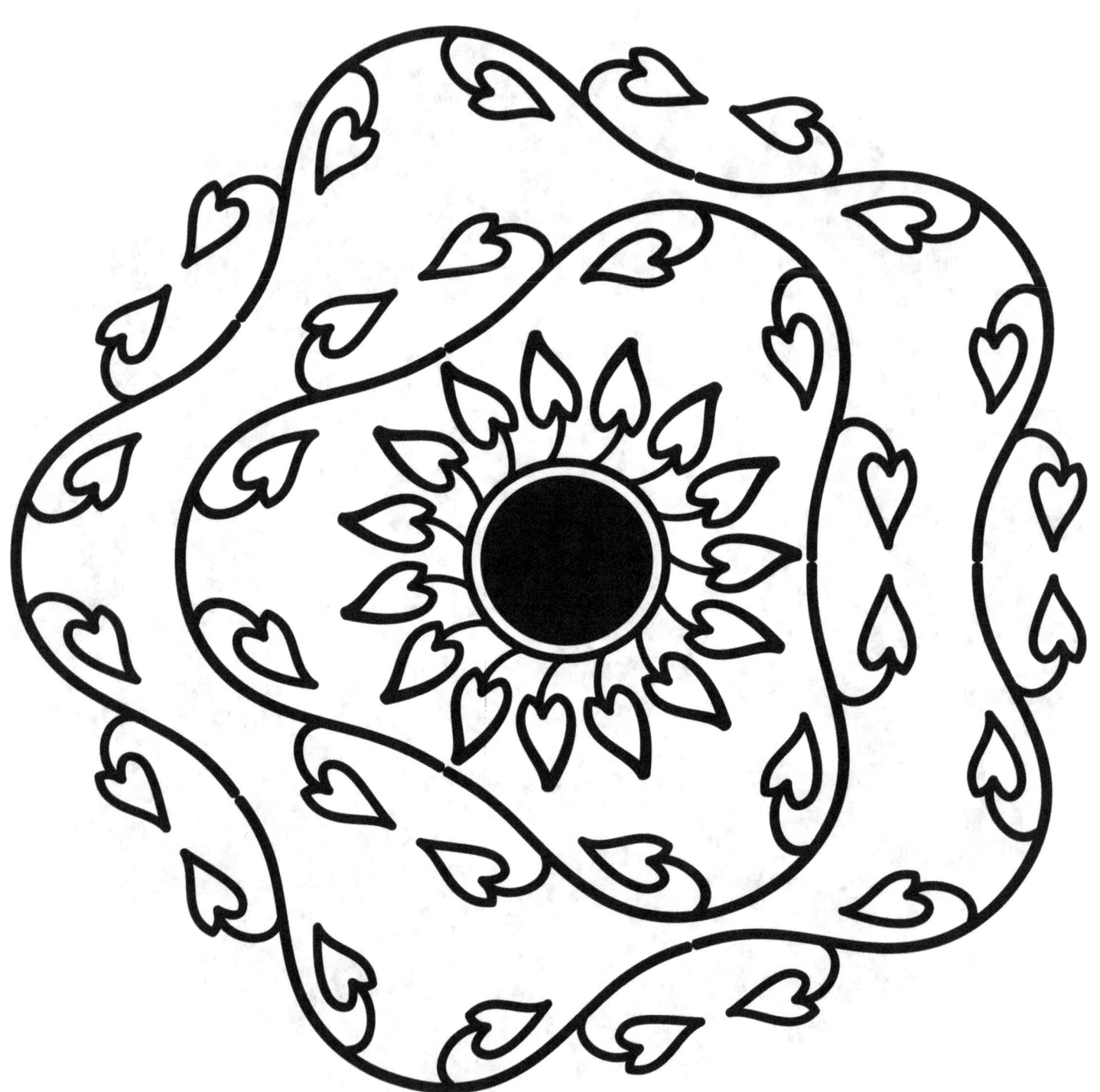

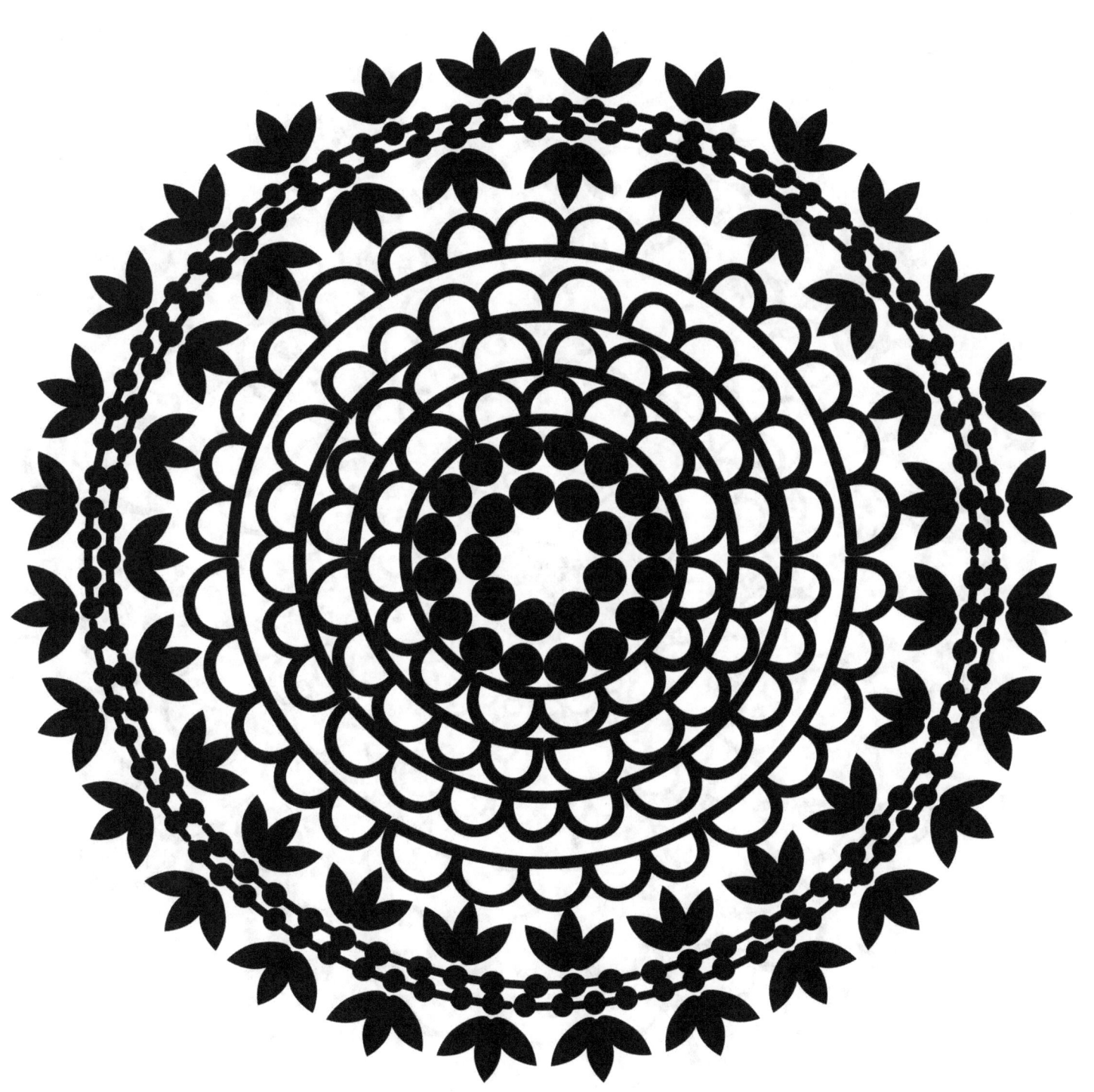

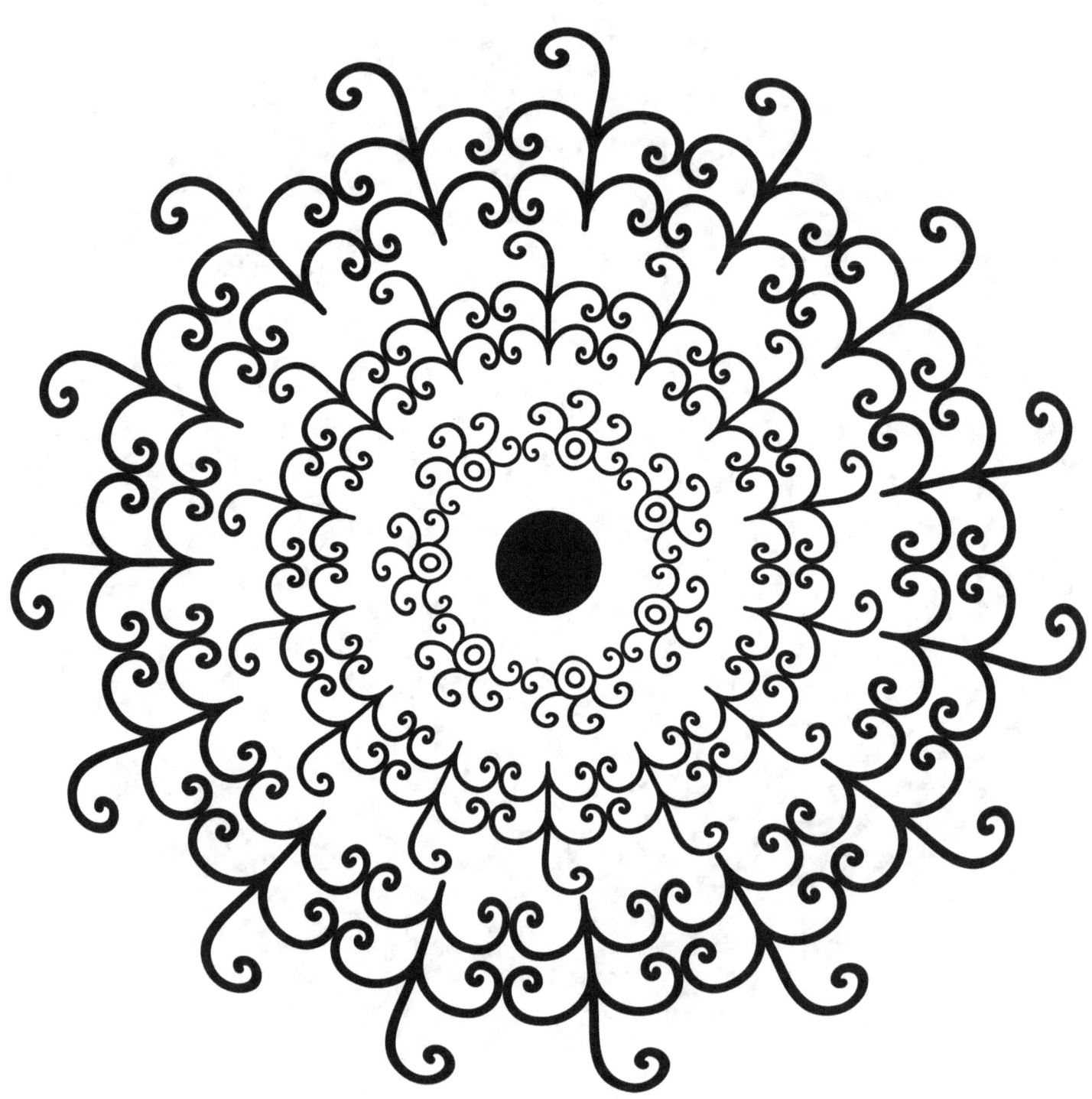

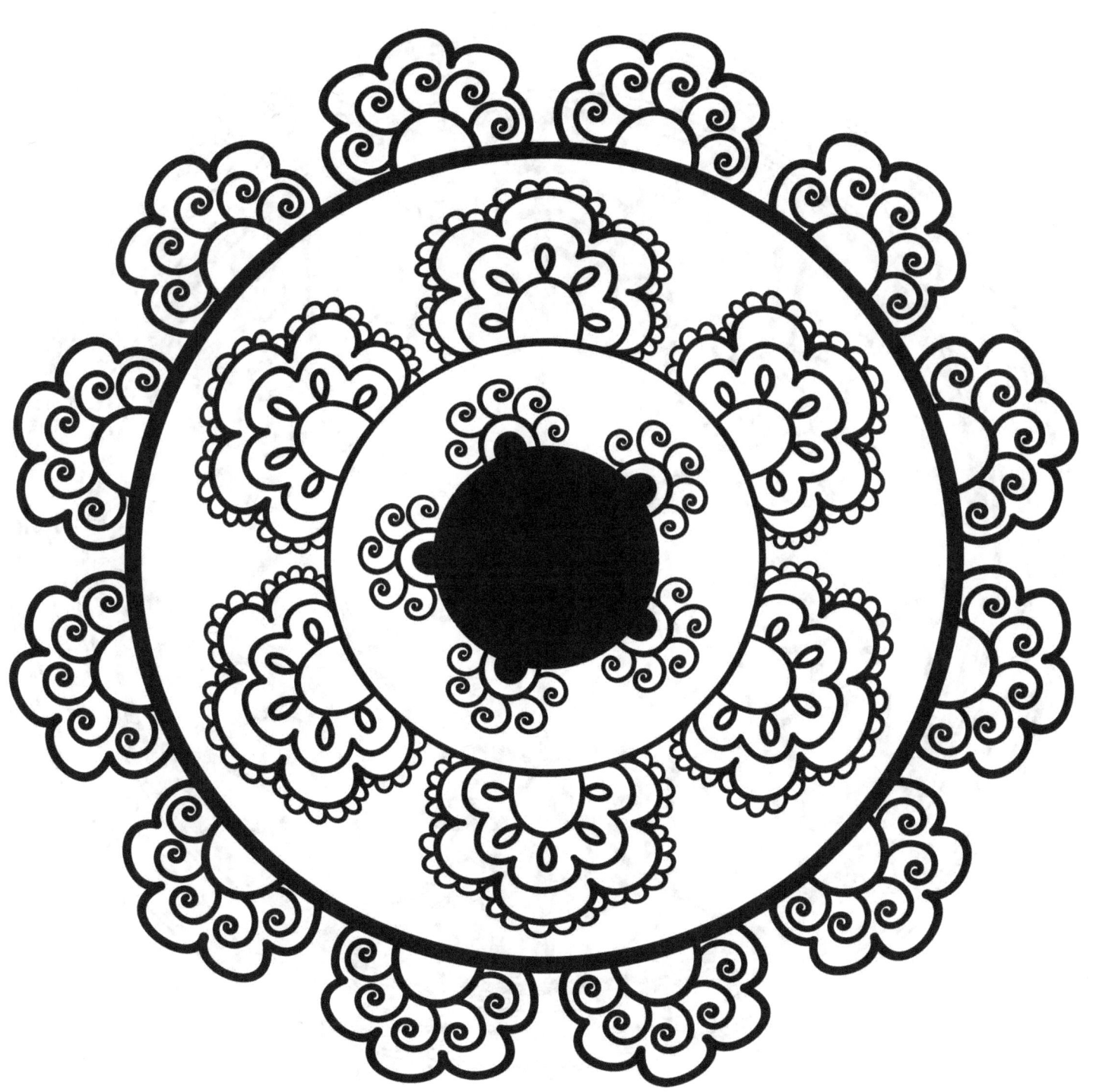

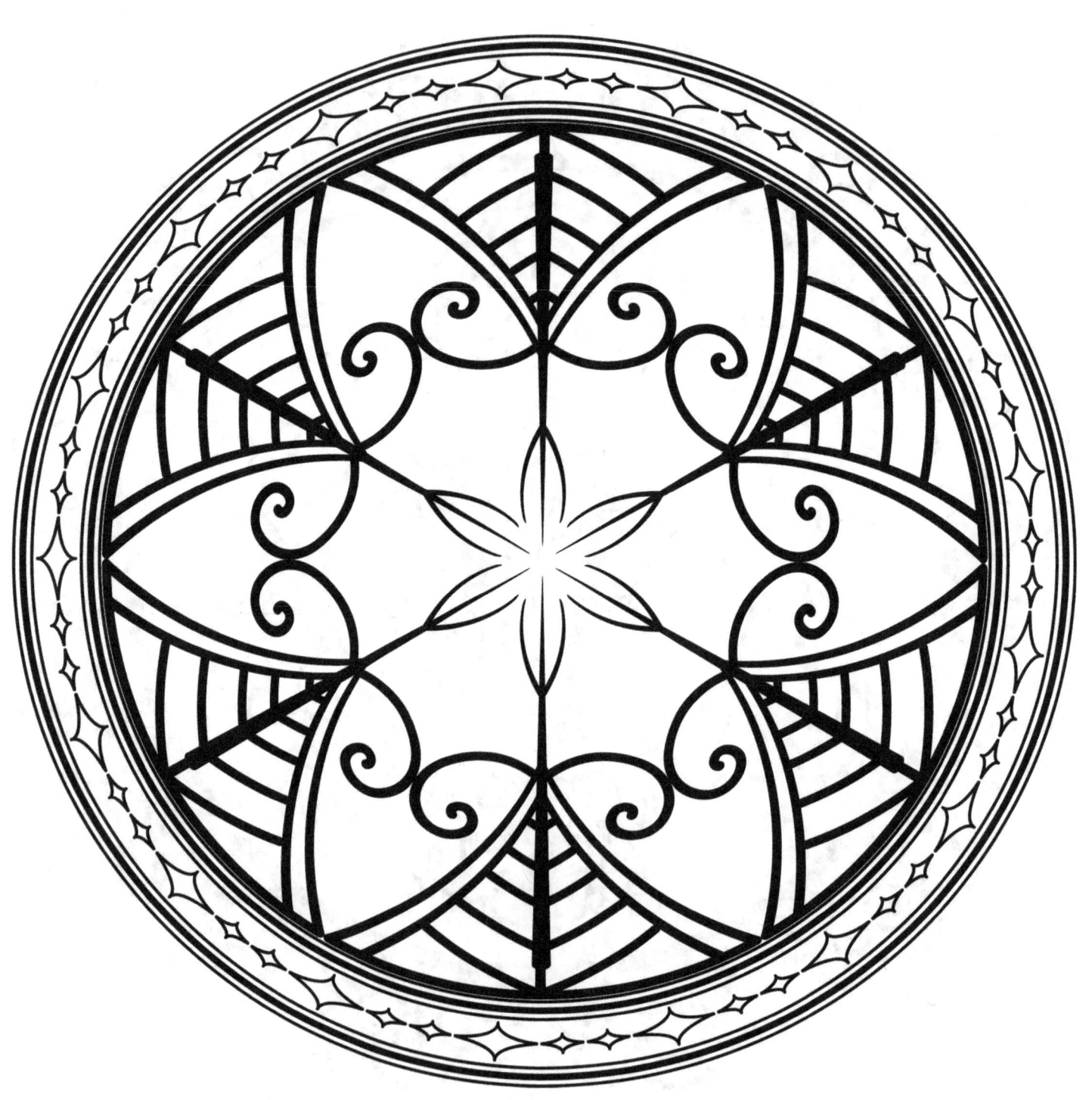

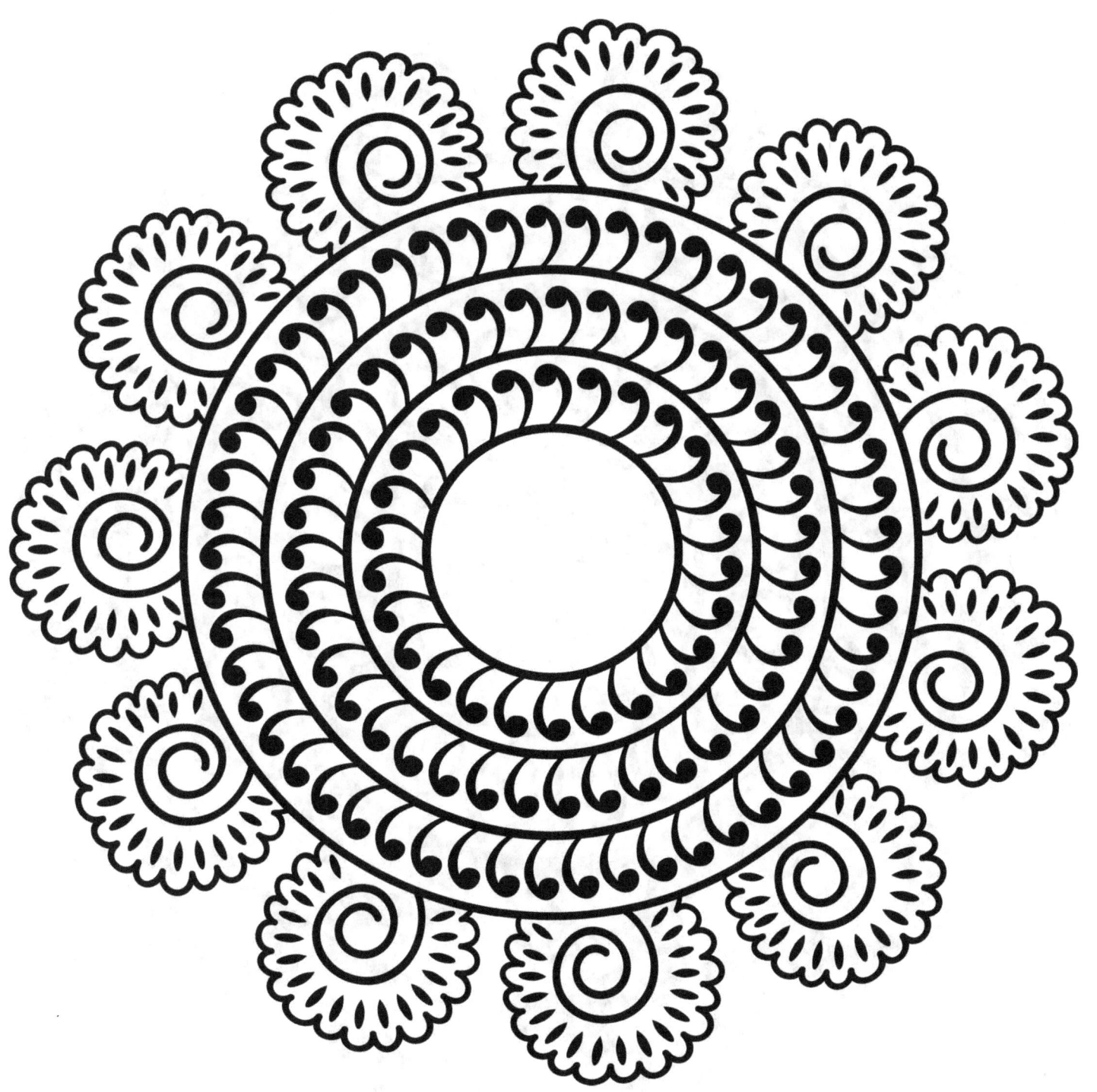

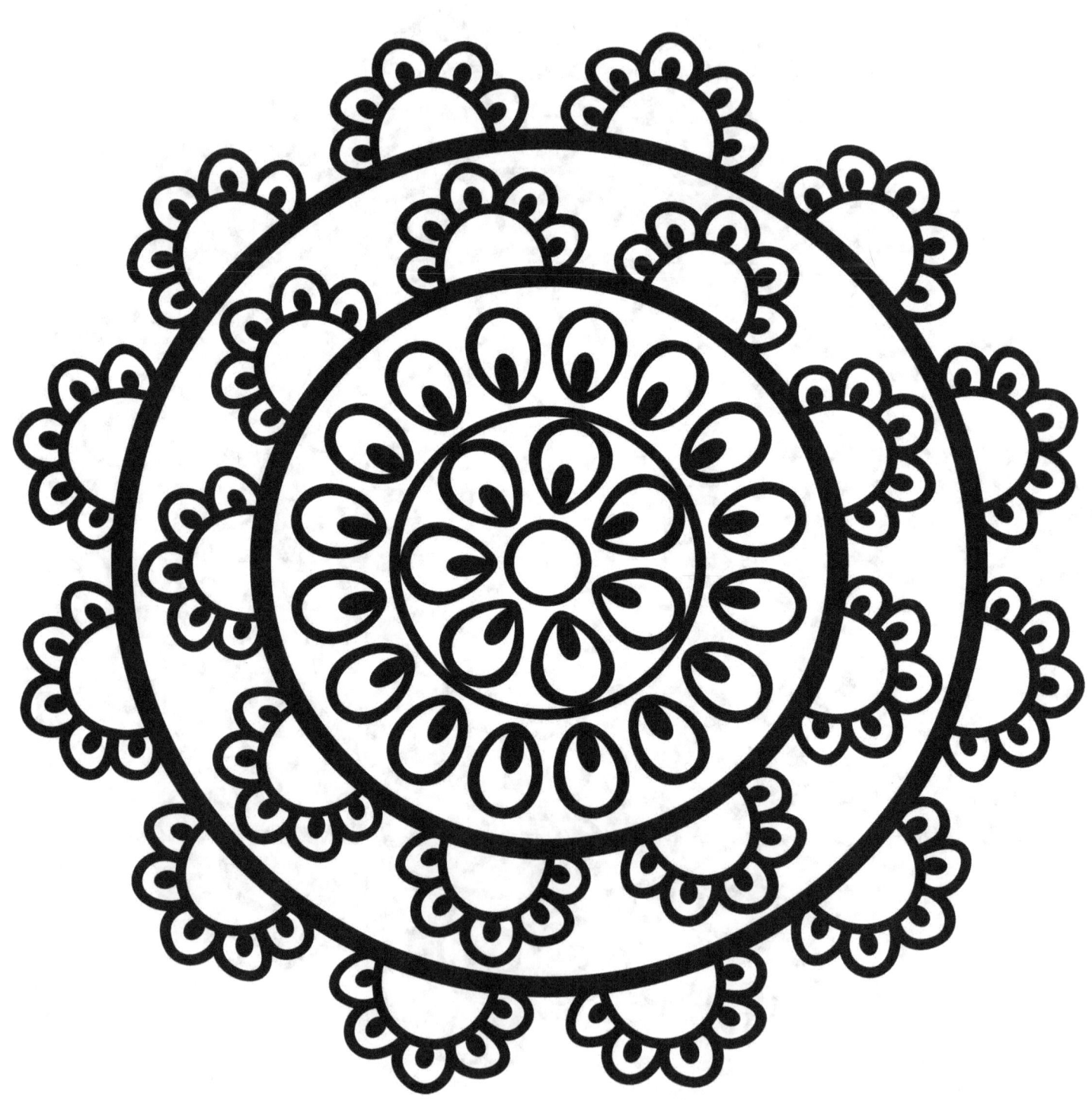

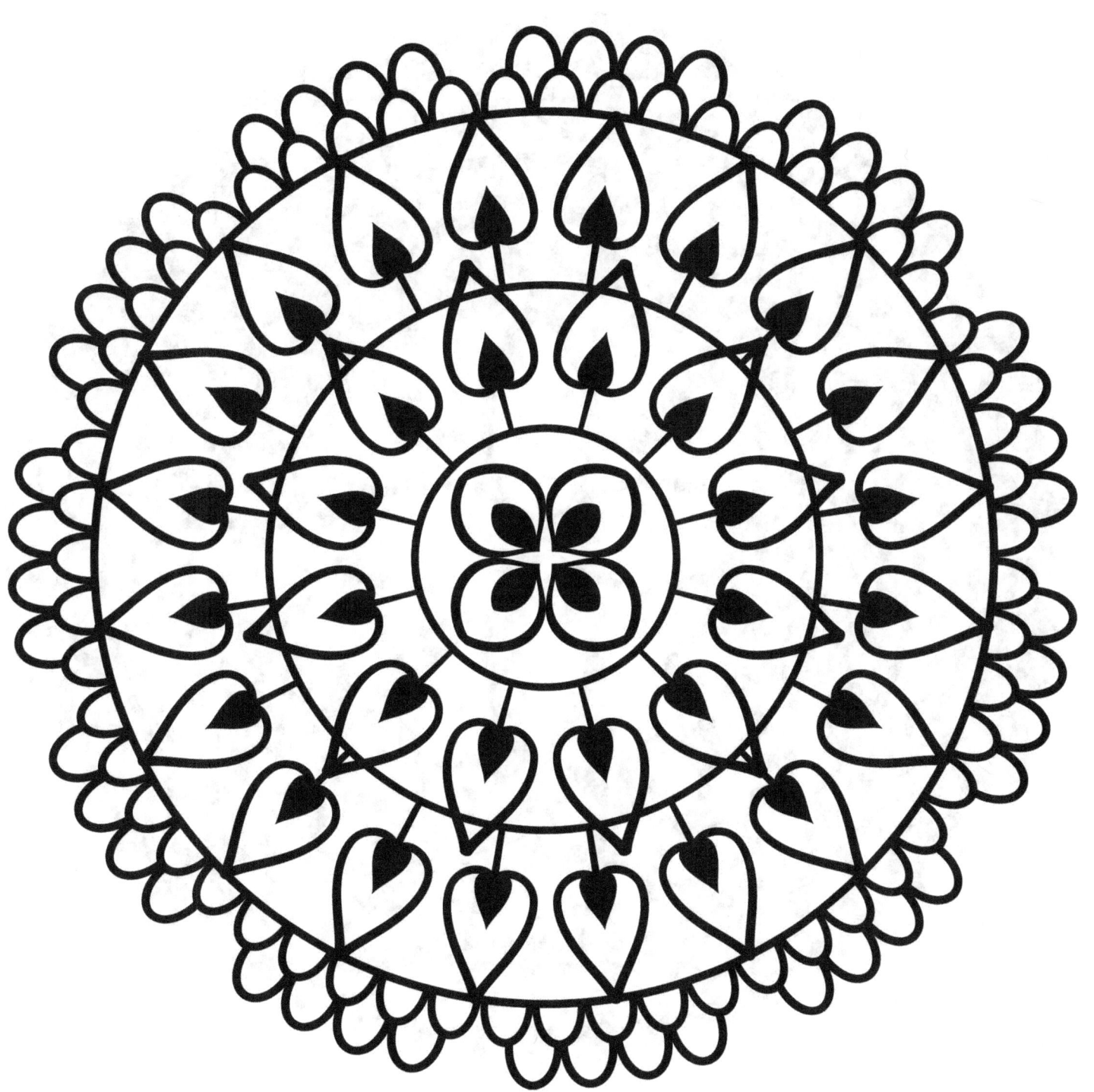

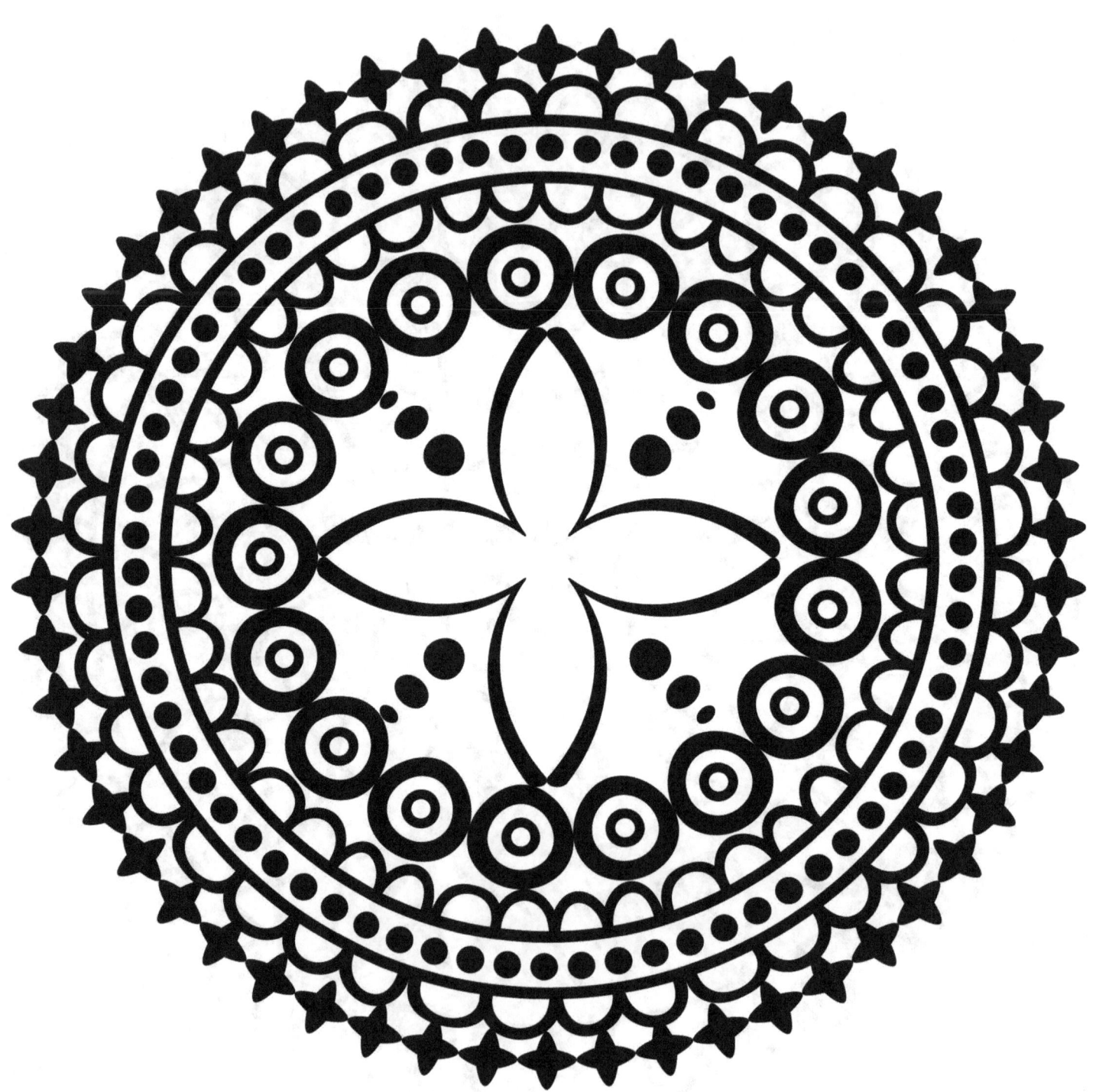

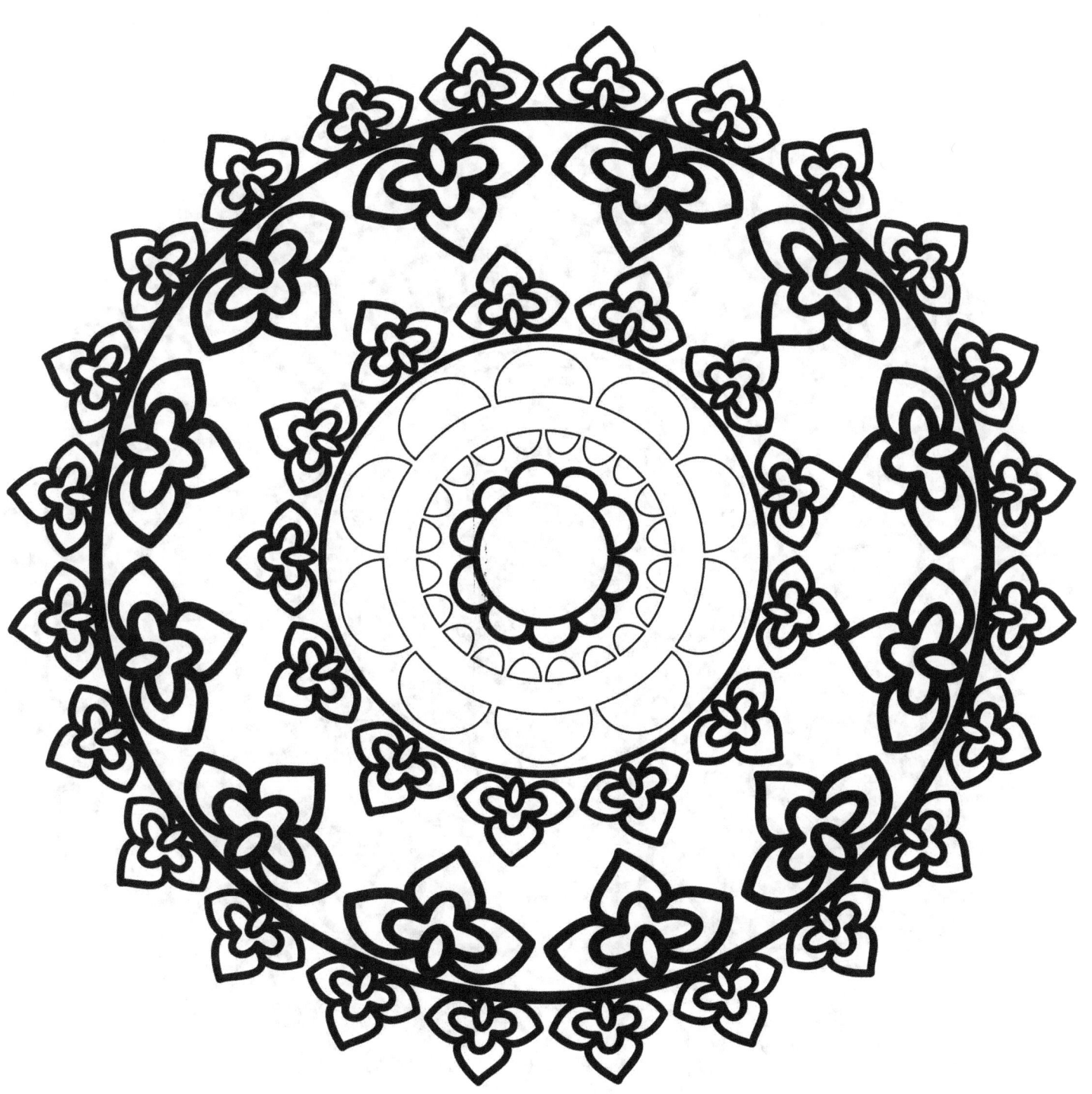

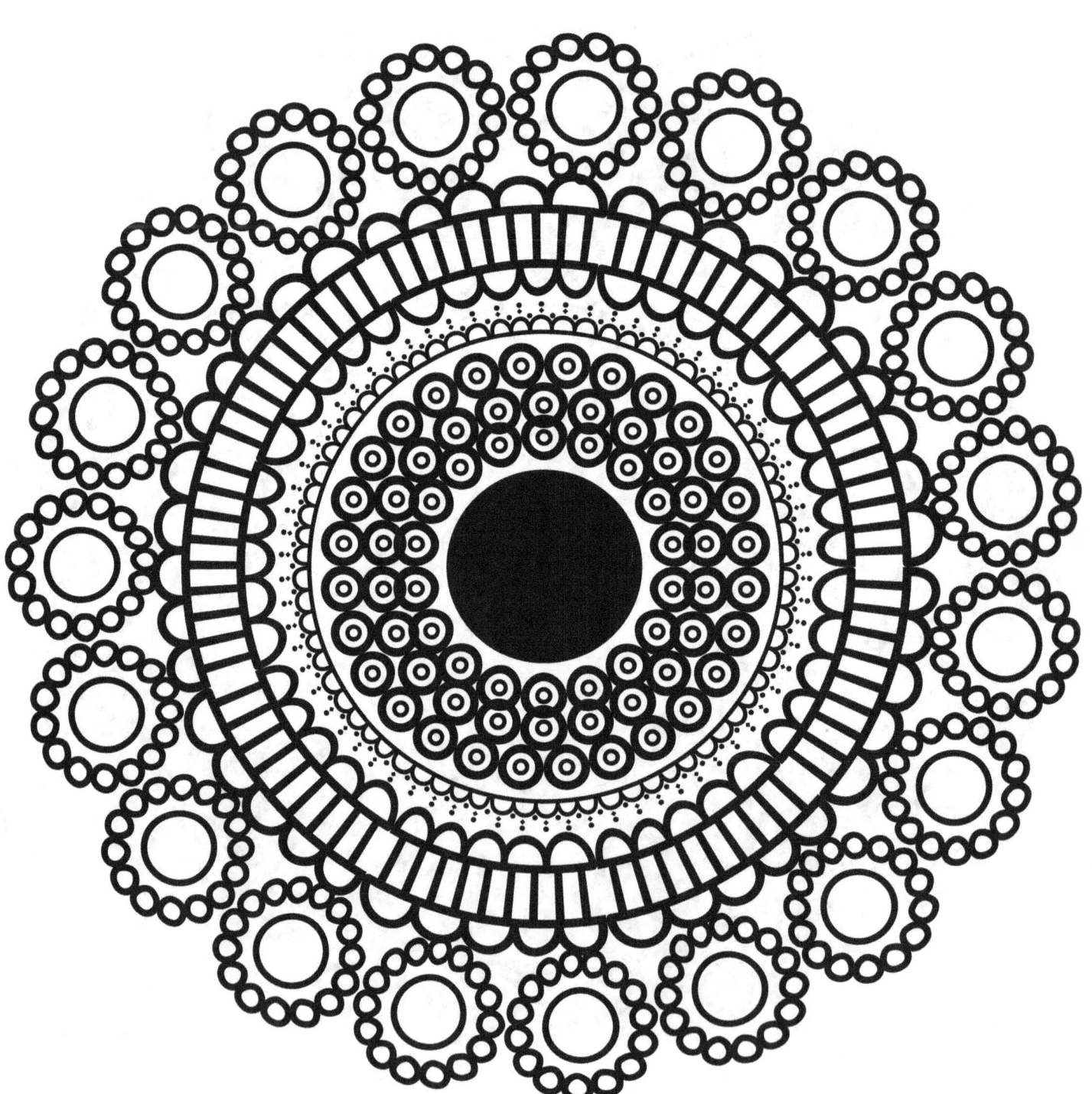

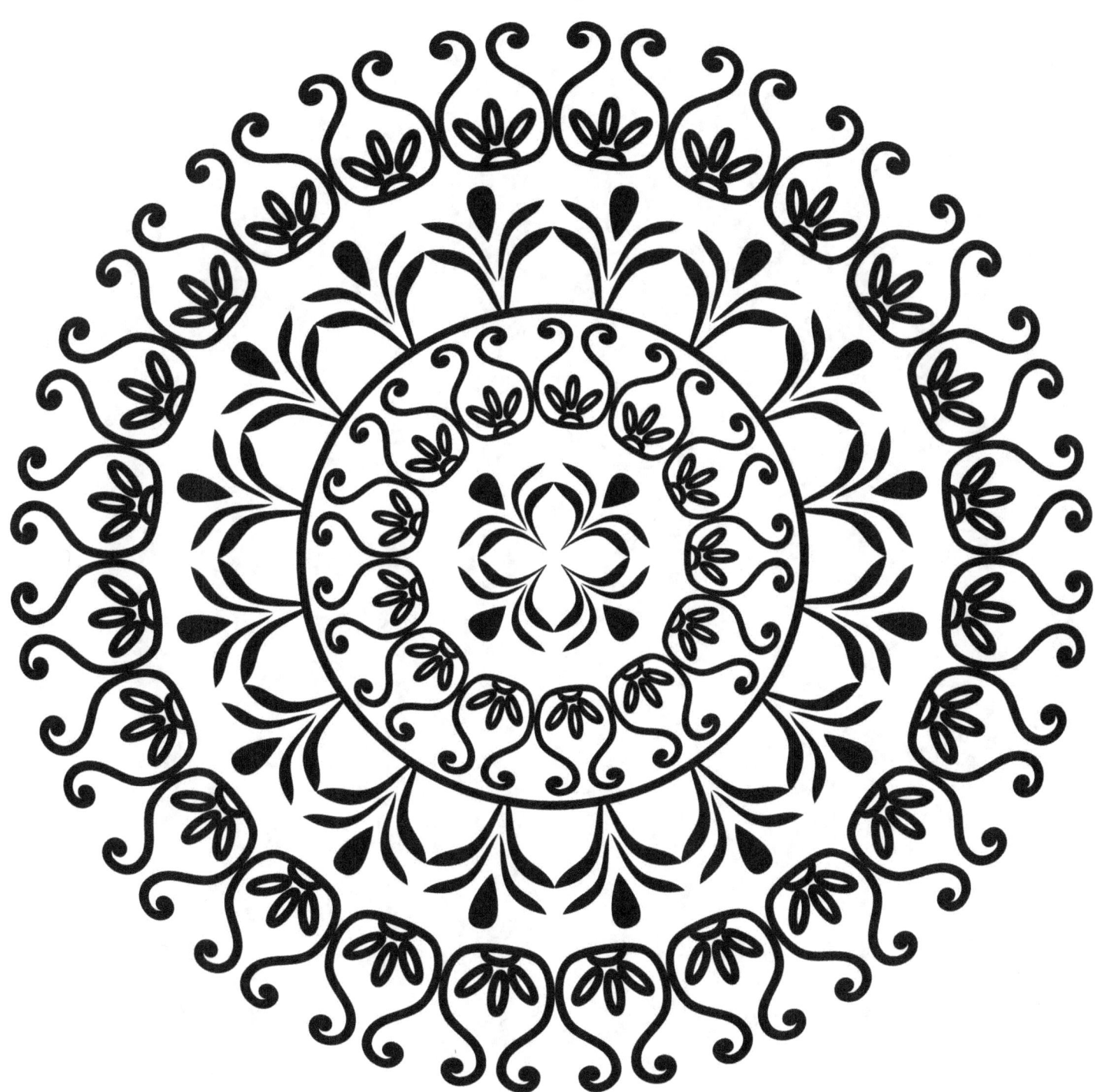

www.ingramcontent.com/pod-product-compliance
Lightning Source LLC
Chambersburg PA
CBHW080912290526
45795CB00007BA/2511